The Rental Roller Coaster
The Ups and Downs of a Successful Landlord

The Rental Roller Coaster

Sandra Allensworth

Published by Sandra Allensworth, 2023.

THE RENTAL ROLLER COASTER

First edition. October 5, 2023.

Copyright © 2023 Sandra Allensworth.

ISBN: 979-8987675854

Written by Sandra Allensworth.

Table of Contents

To the Roswell Slumlord Association and those who want to join. :))

To my friends Addie and Lynn who understand and have been there come hell or high water.

To Marty who supplied the corner and the coffee.

To the Joy Writers who witnessed and encouraged the assembling of this written montage.

Mostly to my Heavenly Father who saw me through it all.

WARNING

This book should, in no way, be considered legal advice. Consult an attorney in your state and county.

Every state, county, and city may have its own laws governing tenant housing.

Likewise, each governing body might have its own way of interpreting each law and regulation.

What I have attempted to do here is show the reader how some laws have been applied in my case and the cases of other landlords.

All of the stories in this book are representational, resembling no one, living or dead. Most of them are my stories. The rest have been related to me by one or another in my support group, otherwise known as my tribe.

I have never been politically correct. Therefore, I will continue to refer to myself as a landlord. Anyway, it is difficult to be a "lady" in this business.

Also, these caveat-The names were changed to protect the guilty, innocent and the unskilled.

Many of my tenants are good and honorable people. Some of them have become friends. This book, however, is a cautionary tale about those who do not play by the same rules.

Foreword

When I lost my third job in five years, it was time to take stock of my life.

I had previously been self-employed, doing fabrication, installation, and repair of window coverings. All of the businesses in a town of forty-eight thousand contracted for me to provide these services. Some of them only used me when their installers or fabricators were not up to the job.

At one point I decided a paying job would give me some job security. I should say that there were only about six places in a one hundred and forty-mile radius dealing in Interior Design. Slim pickings to be sure, but I finally secured a job.

After losing the jobs due to either the closing of the department or the entire business, I realized my skills lay in figuring out solutions to problems and repairing things. I was also skilled in Interior Design. I talked to a real estate agent I knew and was told that since I had neither job nor money, I would not be able to buy any houses for rentals. Hence my predicament.

Being by nature a stubborn person, I studied books on how others across the nation did that very thing. I will say that not all of them worked in my situation. It was trial and error and took a lot of analyzing to figure out what would work for me.

The following information explains how I did what I did and what it entailed. The strategy I adopted may not be for everyone, but it worked for me. I bought seventeen houses in about six years. It took a lot of time, a credit card, and various practical skills to accomplish this, but if I did it, you can too.

After several years in the business a friend of mine, who owns a Real Estate Company, said to me, "I have watched you for several years and I still can't figure out how you did it."

Here is how I did it.

Chapter 1

The Introduction

First of all, let me tell you about a very bosomy friend of mine who complained about excessive perspiration and chaffing in that area. I suggested that she put cornstarch in her bra to relieve the discomfort. When I later had occasion to ask her if my suggestion helped, she replied, "Have you ever had pudding in your bra?" Similarly, while many of the things I am about to tell you may be true universally, I speak only from my personal experiences and those of close friends.

I have researched over one hundred titles on the subject of being a landlord and have not found a single one that deals with the hand-to-hand, down-in-the-ditches kind of things that I address, by example, in this book. I have tried to explain how I have dealt with real issues and life-size problems.

My hope is that you will find that I have done just that using truth, wisdom, and humor. I want you to know upfront what a contractor friend of mine told me early on: an expert is a drip under pressure. I can therefore be considered an expert.

I have owned rentals for about 20 years. They have been rented mostly to hard-working, honest people with jobs such as mechanic, waitress, caregiver, bookkeeper, housekeeper, E.M.T., and teacher. I have also had renters on government assistance. It is my fervent hope that the reader (hereafter referred to as You) can escape some of the expense and anguish that I have gone through.

The purpose of this book is not to teach you about repairs. There are plenty of good television shows, books, and videos for that. I have written this book as if you and I are sitting in my favorite cafe, sharing coffee and advice about this ever-changing business.

In my own defense and by way of explanation, let me say that I was on a very steep learning curve when I bought my first house. Remember that even with the best of intentions you will only get one person's advice from one person's perspective. This is worth repeating.

One person's advice may not be right for you.
When I started this adventure, I would ask three people the same question and weigh the answers. After a time I realized that one person was giving me very bad advice. I don't know if this was from ignorance of the subject or just plain meanness. I asked one landlord how he keeps his income in line with his expenses. He said that he picks up receipts from the parking lot of a large lumber and hardware store. **If the advice is free, take it for what it is worth and consider the source.**

***

I bought two houses from a woman who acquired them when her husband died. She turned the properties over to a property manager. The manager ordered all repairs done by various repairmen, plumbers, and electricians. I also bought two houses from a lady who owned a local business. One of her friends had suggested that she buy rentals as a good investment, to reduce her taxes. She could not do any of the repairs herself and they soon became money pits. By the time I bought them, they were nearly uninhabitable.

Look for people who have received similar bad advice. You might pick up some good bargains. Be very careful when you do this. You are buying a house "as is." It can be very costly if you make a mistake.

***

In New Mexico, a person can purchase a house on a Real Estate Contract. The owner "carries paper," similar to a bank. I have purchased several houses this way. The houses were usually in bad shape, so it was advantageous to the seller to sell them on contract, to someone who knew how to do the repairs and was willing to buy the house "as is." This financial instrument is not available in all states and in others, it may be called by different names.

***

One house I bought this way was in such bad shape that I told the owner that I would buy it, (basically taking over her payments) on two conditions. One was that she go and look at the house so she would know what I was up against, and the other was that I wait three months before starting the payments because it would take me that long to make it fit to rent.

***

At this point, I should say that when I bought houses with no money down, that did not mean that I paid no money at the time of the purchase. Most of the time I offered to pay the closing costs or at least the escrow set up fees. This was an incentive for the owner to exit the ownership without any financial pain. It was usually two hundred to one thousand dollars per unit depending on whether I only did a wrap-around in an escrow account, or if I went through a title company, which is more expensive. Fees differ in each community. Sometimes we split the fees. This was in 2002-2008.

***

A title search is just what it sounds like. When you use a title company, the last page you sign is one stating that if they make a mistake you will not hold them liable. They promise to fix it.

You can go to the County Courthouse and conduct your own search. If you buy a house from someone who bought it through a title company, then you only have to search as far back as that sale to see if there are any liabilities or liens against the property.

Again let me state, consult an attorney. I am telling you what I did and how I did it.

***

Restoring a house to usability is the ultimate in **recycling** and can be very satisfying and financially rewarding but don't think that you can buy a house and a set of golf clubs. Well, I guess you can, but don't expect to spend much time on the golf course. That is not the way this business works.

***

Before you decide to flip houses be sure to talk to your tax person. If you sell a house within a year of buying it, it will probably be considered capital gains. If you keep it for a year or more, it will probably be considered ordinary income and will be taxed at your tax bracket. Assuming that this is for rental purposes, of course. Talk to your tax person.

Chapter 2

Your Support Group

"You make the list, I'll get the gun."—Not really! Just joking!—Sort of. But one time when I was very angry and frustrated, someone in my support group said that to me. It was an effort to sympathize and commiserate with me. And make me smile. When you put very spare minute of your time, your money, and your blood, sweat, and tears into fixing a house and then take the time to go through the selection process in order to find just the right person to trust with your investment, the emotions can be very strong. It is times like this when you really need someone from your support group to boost you up.

***

One time I went with a person from my support group to one of his houses and we found the front door missing, all the other doors and cabinet doors beaten in, all of the switch plates and plug plates broken, and a window shattered. There was a baseball bat propped up against the wall. There was dog feces on the floor and food in the refrigerator.

My friend's knees buckled. I caught his arm before he fell and took him to get some coffee in order to talk him back to sanity. It can be so hard!!!

***

No matter how much your family and friends love you, they cannot understand you and the complaints you have about your tenants. Common questions are, "Didn't you ask for references?" and "Why don't you just evict them?" There are any number of questions designed to make you feel inept. Turn to your support group. They will understand.

When I have complained about something that has upset me my support group audience would laugh at me with commiseration. We don't expect each other to express sympathy. We are tougher than that. We know what it is all about and that we are just venting. Others will get their turn. It is a safe environment to do that. In our own way, we all sympathize. I suppose that it is similar to any other support group.

***

Sometimes you have to decide whether to leave a house empty, and risk having it broken into and vandalized or rent to someone who seems less than ideal as a tenant.

Sometimes the excuses are real. Sometimes they offer no references. I am always suspicious.

1. I have never rented before. Translation- I am an innocent person. Won't you trust me?

2. I have separated and am getting a divorce. Translation- I am a victim. Don't you feel sorry for me?

3. I just moved here from out of town. Translation- I am a responsible citizen. I am here for a new job.

4. I just got my children back and need a larger house. Translation- My kids were taken away from me and now I am trying to be a good parent. Will you help me?

5. I am going to have another baby and need more room. Translation- Please be kind, I need help.

6. My father (mother) is moving in with me. Translation- Aren't I a good daughter/son?

7. My previous landlord sold the house I was living in. Translation- I am just a victim of circumstance.

8. My previous landlord won't fix anything in the house. Translation- How can anyone be so abusive to me? (Maybe they would not pay the rent and the landlord was trying to get rid of them.)

9. This house is closer to my work (school). Translation- Won't you help me get ahead in my life?

These justifications will resurface in future stories in this journal.

***

Having a good place for your Slumlord Association meetings always helps. Did I neglect to mention that some of our local tribe of landlords refer to ourselves as the Roswell Slumlord Association? If you have the name, you might as well use it. Right?

It helps to have in your group a:

1. A retired judge who has rentals.
2. A banker who understands land lording.
3. A Realtor - preferably one who has rentals.
4. A friend - preferably one who has rentals.
5. A restaurateur who will let you commandeer a table.

The group will offer commiseration, usually in the form of a laugh. We know that if we could not take it, we would not be in this business. Laughter is our way of saying; we have been where you are, things will get better, you will get through this, and most of all, it could have been worse.

***

Being a landlord is not just about collecting rent from compliant and grateful tenants. Determine where you are going to collect rent. I prefer to go to the rental house. This gives me a chance to look over the house and the tenant seems to be more chatty this way. I find out what is going on in their lives and maybe get a preview of what I can expect in the future. Job, divorce, illness, pregnancy etc.

***

Are you tough enough? You may think you are but even the best of us gets beaten down and doubts our knowledge, goodness, and sometimes even our humanity. Bad tenants can wear you down emotionally and financially.

***

I firmly believe that there are only two types of people in this world. Adults and Children.

Some grown people get to be children all of their lives.

The following is proof of my assertation.

Chapter 3

In The Black Or In The Red

The IRS usually expects you to have a 10-month rental history for each house. Keeping a renter for a long period of time puts you ahead of the game and makes you more money in the long run. I think this works even though you don't keep the rent current with the market trends.

***

I have had houses empty for several months while I repaired, cleaned, and looked for an acceptable tenant. I have had houses that have been rented for years. I have not raised the rent on those who have been with me for years. They even get a turkey at Thanksgiving. It all evens out.

***

The longer a house sits empty, the greater the chance that it will be broken into or vandalized. I had refrigerators stolen the day after someone moved out. If I think there may be a problem, I take a two-by-four at least forty-four inches long and anchor it across the door, just below the doorknob. Using **square-headed or hex screws** at least three inches long, driven at an angle close to the door frame, will prevent the door from being kicked in. You may be surprised at how often this happens. Be sure to check all of the window locks when a tenant moves out.

***

For some reason, they will not usually break a window to get in, although I had one Plexiglas windowpane removed so the thieves could gain access. They even took it with them when they left. Maybe because they couldn't get the back door open to remove the refrigerator and stove. The front door had two locks on it. A deadbolt is more difficult to kick in. Having the doors blocked probably saved my appliances since they would not fit through the window. It is a good idea to buy a double-keyed deadbolt to install when the house is empty. Otherwise, they can get in through a window and then open the door. I just thought of this. No one who ever got into my houses this way ever thought to remove the door by taking out the hinge pins. Hmm.

***

On this note: Be sure to change out the locks as soon as you take possession of the house. The cheapest way to do that is to always use the same brand. Then all you have to do is
take out the key cylinder and replace it with another one. I always carry extra lock sets.

***

Here is another very good idea: **Do Not Use Slotted or Phillips Screws.** Everyone has those screwdrivers. Use square head, star, or hex head screws. It frustrates and slows down the nefarious fellows.

***

Ten percent of the rent is usually paid to the property manager. This could be forty or fifty percent of your profit if you have a mortgage on the property. Profit is relative since you still have repairs, taxes, and insurance to consider. Financial advisers will tell you to pay cash when you buy a rental property but if you have no job or a low-paying job that is not an option. At least paying cash wasn't possible in my case. Of course, buying a rental property under these conditions is risky and foolhardy at best.

***

A property manager will call his repair service people. You can usually do that.
Some people don't like to be bothered with such things. It is a lifestyle choice. You have to figure out your own tolerance level for aggravation and inconvenience; and of course, your financial situation.

THE RENTAL ROLLER COASTER

One property manager of my acquaintance was talking in his office with a landlord client. The phone rang and a tenant told him that there was an awful racket on the roof. The property manager immediately called his maintenance man and sent him to the address. Before the maintenance man arrived, the tenant called back and said, "Never mind. The noise stopped. The air conditioner is in the backyard now."

***

I purchased a house and started to work on it. The neighbor came over to make my acquaintance and explained that the reason there was no screen door was because there had been a wrought iron screen/security door on the house but because the screen was torn, the maintenance people had removed it. He explained that since the tenant was on government assistance, if the screen door had ever had a screen, and did not at the time of inspection, then maintenance men had the choice of repairing or removing it. They chose to remove the door and give it to him. Or so he said.

***

Same house, different problem: Two weeks after the purchase of said house, the ceiling in the hallway fell in, flooding the area. An inspection of the evaporative cooler on the roof revealed that whoever had last repaired it had not done so correctly.

Once the ductwork filled up with water, it soaked through the ceiling. This caused the mess which I now had to clean up before I could repair the damage. Note here that the property manager did not inspect the repair work. His job was to order the work done, pay the repair bill, deduct that amount from the rent money and send the balance to the owner.

***

You might as well rent some equipment instead of maintaining and storing it yourself. Even shampooers. That way you do not have to store, maintain, or repair equipment, which also eats into your valuable time. It depends on whether you want to save time or money.

I had a rather expensive shampooer which a tenant wanted to borrow. There is a reservoir for hot water to scrub the floor and then the vacuum action sucks up the dirty water. Very nice. I made the mistake of letting her use it. When she returned it, it was in two pieces. She said, "It just happened. It's not my fault." Three hundred fifty dollars in 2010. She was on public assistance and government housing so taking her to court would have been futile. Don't loan your equipment.

***

You can hardly get a deposit large enough to cover the damages that can be caused by a tenant. In New Mexico, if you hold a deposit larger than the rent, you have to keep it in a separate account and pay interest on it. Check the laws in your state.

***

By the time you pay someone, (or do it yourself) to rake the yards, reseed and water the lawn, haul dirt to fill the holes, repair the fences, clean and do repairs on the house, you will be out quite a bit of time or money. It is beginning to sound like a losing proposition, isn't it? Talk to your tax person.

***

I never did this but why not open an XXX Repair and Cleaning business? You would have more paperwork and have to file with the city and Feds but XXX could charge you, the landlord, for their services. Since you work for XXX your labor would be paid for. In New Mexico you cannot deduct your own labor on your taxes. I assume this is a Federal law. Better ask your accountant about this.

***

Some people set up their rentals on a twenty-seven-and-one-half year depreciation. This will shelter your income but just remember that this will be recouped by the IRS when you sell. You will have to pay back all of your depreciation. By selling the houses on a contract you can stretch this out and so not be hit with the recoup of all the depreciation at once. This may or may not be an advantage to you. I have asked my tax accountant if there is any way to shelter my income. The last time I asked, he placed his hand on my shoulder and said in a commiserating tone of voice, "Not legally."

***

The one thing that gets me is that if I do a remodel or put on a roof, I have to put it on depreciation and apply a portion of it to my taxes each year for ten years. This is even though I have had all the expenses in one year.

***

When selling on contract, you should probably get a higher interest rate than the banks. If the prospective buyer could get a loan, they would have already done that. You are assuming the risk of a buyer who may not have good credit. This may not always be true but enter at your own risk! Also, the laws regarding real estate contracts are very different in each state. Consult an attorney.

***

I have been told by some long-time landlords, who have sold houses on contract, that the houses are frequently returned to them after about five to seven years. It will take a lot of tact to get this handled. I know of one buyer who bought a repossessed house from the bank and found out that the previous owner had poured cement down the drainpipes. Because the cement set up before it went very far down the drain, he was able to chip out the cement and replace the p-trap without having to do much plumbing. Some people have a mean and vindictive spirit.

***

I have had two houses returned to me (2019) so far. One was after a year. They never paid on time and accused me of "tricking them into buying." The other was after two years. They said that an aunt had willed them a house, so they did not need mine. Both times it cost me several thousand dollars to return the houses to their previous condition.

***

Consider how much you will gain by raising the rent compared to your tax bracket. You should also consider what it will cost you if a good tenant decides that the increase in the rent is more than he or she can afford. Not raising the rent will certainly make your tenants happy and therefore you will probably not have so many vacancies.

Gamblers call that "leaving something on the table." No empty house, advertising, showing property, interviewing, background checks, cleaning fees. It all adds up and takes not only money but time. Be careful because if the rents are very much out of line with the local market, the IRS might question your motives.

***

As a house gets run down, I lower the rent to keep it rented through another renter. This gets me a little more mileage out of the house before I have to put a lot of money into it. Some tenants are not as particular as others. Putting new flooring in a house, when compared to the monthly rent and the time lost, gives you an idea of the actual expense.

***

When I have had a house for several years and it comes up empty, I sometimes do an overhaul and then sell it. It is easier to sell an older house if it presents well. This seems to be especially true if you have to replace the roof. Consider how much depreciation you have left on your tax schedule.

***

Tile is another option, but it makes a house colder and noisier. I have never had a tenant who would keep the grout clean. If you do tile, use a dark-colored grout. Sealing the tile helps but it needs to be done every 6-12 months, depending on the traffic. I tile the kitchen, baths, hall, living room and dining area. I usually carpet the bedrooms. Tenants don't usually eat in the bedroom so the carpet stays decent for a longer period than it would in the living room.

They will sometimes drag furniture and drop it on the tile, cracking it. But they also drag furniture across the carpet, tearing it. I use a vinyl tile product that looks like wood. It costs more than carpet, but it lasts longer. Choose your poison.

***

One landlord advised me to furnish my houses and then raise the rent by fifty to seventy-five dollars per month. I never thought that would be a good idea. If you rent it furnished then you are responsible for maintenance, cleaning, and replacement. I suppose you could advertise it as "partially furnished" until it has all been destroyed. Most people who rent houses have their own furniture. Seldom do they have a stove or refrigerator but almost all of them have big screen televisions and gaming devices. Go figure.

***

You may not be able to charge enough rent to cover your expenses at first. If you have a mortgage, taxes, insurance, an empty unit, or the occasional hot water heater and HVAC repair, be prepared to do some of the repairs yourself. If you don't, you should have a job to help cover your expenses. Economically, what helped me the most was that, after I bought a few houses, I no longer owed any taxes because of the expenses and depreciation on the properties. The trick here is trying to keep everything even.

***

I keep my rent about fifty to one hundred dollars below the current market. This keeps me from having so much turnover. The tenants usually appreciate me for doing this and return the favor by doing simple repairs and keeping me informed if they are going to be late on the rent. Of course, some do not.

***

Some in my support group charge top dollar for their units, but those are the first to come up empty. Some of the landlords supply water and lawn care. You just have to structure your business to fit your preferences, situation, and disposition. It has been my experience that when I pay the water bill, the tenant has no incentive to conserve water. I have found water running down the street, leaking wading pools, hoses attached to evaporative air conditioners, and in one instance a large above-ground swimming pool, filled with water, under the shelter of a pole barn.

***

I normally do not charge a late fee if the tenants tell me in advance that they will be a little late and do not abuse the privilege. It helps develop good relationships. If they wait until the rent is due and I have arrived to collect the rent, they are charged. Turnover will cost you in lost rent and cleaning plus the aggravation of having to go through the selection process to find a new tenant. Maybe you happen to like that sort of thing. I don't.

***

If there is an emergency in the house, such as a lack of water, et cetera, you are required to supply alternative housing while the situation is resolved.

I was out of town when a tenant asked her neighbor to go into the attic to take the cookie sheet off the evaporative cooler. This keeps cold air from blowing into the house in the winter. He stepped on the water line and flooded the house.

I had to provide her with a motel room while it was fixed. Legal responsibility is hard to affix and if the tenant has no money, what difference does it make? She was on government housing assistance and getting her out would have cost me more money than getting her a cheap motel room and fixing the damage.

***

Some people rent while they save money to buy a home. I will not rent to anyone who does not sign a one-year contract. In a small town, if a home gets a reputation for people moving in and out, it begins to look as though there may be something wrong with the home. This is, of course, just my opinion. The one time I did that for a niece, she left without paying the last month's rent.

***

Short-term rentals may work for you. During most of my time as a property owner, I had a full-time job, so it was not advantageous for me to have tenants moving in and out every few months. Also, cleaning up after people puts me in a bad mood so it works better for me if they don't move very often.

Chapter 4

Raising a Good Tenant

I used to tell my tenants not to mistake my kindness for weakness. This sage comment was always met with a blank stare, so I quit confusing them. When I began this business, I was under the impression that all you had to do was be nice to people and they would be nice to you. This is not always the case.

***

Remember this: A Rental Agreement is NOT an Adoption Agreement!

***

I recall one couple well. They rented a very nice four bedroom, two bath, recently remodeled house. They tried to get the upper hand by demanding that one thing and then another be fixed, painted, or replaced. They said that their uncle was a plumber and gave reasons for me to hire an electrician. They said that their uncle was a landlord and they knew their rights, that the house was not safe, and that I should be reported.

They volunteered that the uncle would fix things cheaply. When I got tired of discussing things with them, I told them that if they were out of the house within the week, and they left everything as they found it, I would give them back their rent and deposit. They got upset and said that I was trying to evict them. Once I had their attention they backed down. Of course, when I eventually had to evict them, they trashed the place.

Be firm. Do not let them intimidate you. If things get really ugly, I tell them that I will not have an adversarial relationship with my tenants and that they will not be happy in my house so they should make arrangements to leave within the week. Stay strong.

***

THE RENTAL ROLLER COASTER

After you have chosen a tenant, it sometimes feels like you have adopted a child. They may come with bad habits and will crowd the line of common sense to test you. They may start out very recalcitrant. Some do not respond well to kindness. They perceive it as a sign of weakness. In order to maintain some kind of equilibrium in the landlord-tenant relationship, they need to be shown that there are consequences.

***

If it is hard to maintain good feelings toward some tenants just remember this: there is such a thing as average intelligence. This means that half the population is below average intelligence. It is hard to tell without having them tested. I don't think this is legal. :) Some of them are deliberately obtuse. They are all children of the Universe.

We just don't know which planet they come from. Maybe the planet of Bat Crap Crazy. Some of them are disguised as idiots. They may have been put in your path for you to teach and help or maybe to try your soul. You could be a better person for the encounter. So could they. We are all part of His Master Housing Plan.

***

I had a tenant tell me that the water had been turned off because she could not pay the bill. She was on her way to get a dollar hamburger and a dollar soda for her child because he did not like the food that was in the refrigerator. I pointed out to her that the two dollars she said that she spent every day for this meal would have paid her water bill. She seemed very surprised when I pointed out the math. Apparently, she could not figure that two dollars times thirty days equals a sixty-dollar water bill. Sometimes they act like children. Just remember that you only rent to them. You did not take them to raise.

***

Some renters never seem to bother you for anything, and others are in constant need and won't fix anything. I had one tenant call me to unstop a toilet and mop up the mess on the floor. I told him that he needed to plunge the toilet and

21

mop up the mess himself. He said that he did not have a plunger. I suggested that he buy one. Really!!

***

If you find a mattress in the backyard, look up. I failed to do so and the end result was a damaged roof. I asked the tenant why the mattress was in the backyard. She said that the kids were using it like a trampoline. During one of my drive-bys, I saw the kids playing on the roof. I told her to make sure that the children did not get on the roof. She assured me that they were not, they just went to get a toy that landed up there, and they were only bouncing on the mattress. I thought, all right, a poor boy's toy. I did not like it but if you remember- somewhere in this book, I mentioned that I require the front yard to look nice but am not so particular about the backyard because you have to pick your battles and this was not one that I chose.

After I finally had to evict them, among the things I checked was the roof. There were numerous shingles missing. When I was on the roof replacing them, another helpful neighbor came by and offered this bit of information. The children would climb on the roof and, riding a skateboard, sail down the roof, landing on the previously mentioned mattress. I wonder what liability I would have had if one of the chowderheads had broken a limb.

***

If you find graffiti on your house or fence, paint over it immediately. If you don't it will become a message board for every gang member in town. You will have to use Kilz or an oil-based paint to cover the writing and artistry. I have had to paint over signs, words and obscene pictures.

***

When I first rent to a tenant, I frequently leave some small thing undone and promise to be back in a week or two. This gives me a chance to see how they live: such as putting dirty dishes in the sink with food on them.- It will stop up the pipes. Cutting food on the counter.- This damages the counter. This type of common sense argument will not affect them but telling them that it transfers germs and could make them sick, might influence their behavior. Make it personal, you might get their attention. You just have to keep weeding them out until you either get them trained or get rid of them. Some people live very hard in a house.

***

Against my better judgment, I rented a three-bedroom house to two young men. I don't know to this day if they fooled me or if the partnership just fell apart. Once one of them decided to get married, he failed in his financial responsibilities. Anyway. - There was a brick planter at the front door. I purchased flowers to fill it, thinking that since this was their first home away from their moms, they would appreciate the homey touch.

Silly me.

They not only did not water the flowers, but they dismantled the brick planter and used the bricks for steppingstones to the front door. I asked them why and was told that they needed steppingstones. I pointed out that there was gravel there for that purpose. Unless you have seen the blank look that a tenant gives you when you try to reason with them, you cannot understand the frustration of a landlord.

***

One time I went by and saw two lawn chairs on the roof of the porch. Apparently, they climbed up the metalwork on the porch, got on the roof, drank beer and surveyed the neighborhood. Eventually, I had to start eviction proceedings. They vacated the house, leaving it filthy. There were columns of empty beer cans in each corner of two rooms. There was a paper border picturing beer cans tacked around the upper walls of the living room. There was a fifty-gallon trash can in the laundry room and another right outside of the back door. They were both filled to overflowing with pizza boxes and empty beer cans. The laundry room floor was littered with pizza boxes which appeared to be glued to the floor with spilled beer.

***

Let me interject something here- Federal law prevents the Post Office, employers, utility companies and others from telling you where the ne'er do wells have moved. If you don't have that information, you can't file against them in court in order to get a judgment for unpaid rent or damages. Your government at work.

***

Tenants occasionally come with bad habits and will crowd the line of common sense to test you. They may start out as very surly and recalcitrant. They may be argumentative and belligerent. I don't know if they are born that way or if they learned this conduct somewhere in their lives. Some do not respond well to kindness. They need to be shown that there are consequences for their actions in order to establish some equilibrium in the landlord-tenant relationship.

***

When you are trying to find good tenants, the first thing that you need to remember is that most people live from one paycheck to another. Any action on your part can have serious consequences for them. That is not a reason to let them take advantage of you but, at least in my case, it sometimes tempers my actions.

***

If the applicants are less than you might hope for, you have to decide whether to take the chance of leaving the house empty or selecting someone who is not what you would prefer. Leaving the house vacant exposes the house to vandalism and the theft of appliances and copper wiring. People will also steal air conditioning units, refrigerators, stoves, doors, light bulbs, smoke detectors, and plumbing fixtures. Some people will pull the copper out of the walls and circuit box. Vacating tenants will also sometimes do these things. Especially if they have been evicted.

***

I called the police when I found a refrigerator missing after a move-out. The tenant was in a wheelchair and had caregivers. When the officer asked for her name, I gave it to her and she said, "I know her. I have arrested her."

"Are you sure? She is in a wheelchair."

"That's her. I arrested her for marijuana use."

"Well, that explains some things."

***

I had another house that did not have a bad reputation but had a neighbor with anger issues and a bad attitude. I rented the house to youthful newlyweds and thought everything would be fine. The girl's mother even called to thank me for renting to them because no one else would, because of their ages.

Within a week they called me and said that the neighbor had thrown a brick through their car window. I don't know why I was the first person they called. I went to the house to investigate and called the police. Denial by the neighbor led to a standoff.

The next week the tenants called and said that they were leaving. They left no forwarding address and did not ask for the deposit back. They simply fled. I wish them well.

***

This a story about a screwball that I rented to when I was managing some houses for a landlord—For Free. The owner was about to lose everything because he could not deal with the tenants. The fact that he was a heavy marijuana user might have had something to do with it. I did not know this at the time.

Anyway, I will call the tenant Daft for reasons that will become abundantly clear. I rented a two-bedroom house to Daft and she moved in with her dogs. She antagonized the neighbors for a lot of reasons, not the least of which was her constant complaining.

Daft bought a car. The car did not run very reliably. She also could not register it because she did not have a title. One day she got a ticket, which required that she to go to Municipal Court. Her car would not start. She visited a neighbor and asked for a ride to court. The neighbor refused. When Daft left their yard, she took their weed eater.

The neighbor called the police and Daft was arrested. She was put in a psychiatric facility for evaluation. I learned about this when I found an unknown woman in her house, going through her things. She said that Daft had asked her to get her glasses and meds because she was in jail.

When her trial date came up, I talked to her attorney. The judge was not going to let her out until her attorney told the judge that I would be responsible for her. She was not a danger to herself or others, she simply had trouble functioning. She told me that she was moving to Texas, and I lost track of her.

Many months later I saw her at a shopping mall. She was trying to get a ride somewhere. She was in a wheelchair. I found out that she was homeless, and the police had picked her up again. They gave her a couple of days free at a local motel.

I told her that I had a house I was working on and that if she wanted to stay there, she was welcome. I put her in the house and gave her boxes of food, bedding, dog food and other things.

When she received her government check, she went across the street and talked those people into renting her a room. Ka-ching. They saw free money. I asked for my key back and she complied.

When I went to work on the house several days later, I found it odd that the blinds were open when I had closed them, and I spotted cigarette ashes by the window. I changed the locks.

The neighbor came by and told me the rest of the story. Daft moved in and was not a good tenant. She soon started asking for a return of the rent money so she could buy cigarettes and things.

Within the month they kicked her out of the house. She started spending the night in my house, using a copy of the key she had returned to me. This was one time when I did not change the lock. I should have!

Daft came by one day and wanted me to help her find a home. I made an effort to get her located but she did not like her options. I never heard from her again. I shake my head, at me and her.

***

That reminds me of another instance where I was working **for free** for the same landlord. He was not able to deal with confrontations so when the tenants said they did not have the rent; he did not know what to do about it. I felt sorry for him because it looked like he was going to lose his properties. I was taking care of his four-plex and had cleaned up and rented each unit as I finished it.

There was one last efficiency apartment that I was repairing and cleaning. I noticed that there appeared to be someone using the apartment because I found cereal bowls in the sink and the oven was warm. There were also some blankets which were spread out behind the sofa. I threw them in the trash along with some clothes and personal items. I changed the lock on the door.

In a day or two I noticed that the lock had been jimmied. The items from the dumpster were again in the apartment. I called the owner and he asked me to take care of it. I told him that this was a legal issue and since I was not his property manager he needed to be there when I called the police and made arrangements for a police visit. I called the police and asked them to show up at six o'clock AM the next day. They showed up, as did the owner. He introduced himself, said that I was acting on his behalf, and then went to hide out of sight.

The police knocked on the door. No answer. They tried the door. Locked. They said that no one was there and started to leave. I suggested that they announce themselves louder. They did. No answer. I asked them to break the door in since the lock had been jimmied and barely caught. They said they couldn't do that. I stepped forward and said that I would. I pushed the door with my shoulder, and it flew open.

I felt a tug on my shirt tail and was pulled back out the door. One officer told me to step back and they both went in. I followed. Gun drawn, the lead officer said, "Get out of there! Get out of there, NOW!" Soon a man emerged from the closet. The officers took him outside.

One officer patted him down and asked the squatter what was under his pants. "A colostomy bag," he replied. The officer recoiled. I was asked what I wanted to do with him. I said that I would call the owner. He showed up few minutes later and said that he wanted to turn the squatter loose if he promised to never show up there again. He was let go. I cleaned the apartment.

***

Sometimes a renter thinks because they pay the rent on time it makes them a good tenant. They will then use that as leverage to get concessions from you. Like expecting you to ignore the fact that they have a dog or don't take care of the yards or alley. It is best to make them understand that paying the rent on time and taking care of your property is the minimum that you expect of them. Hold the line. Remind them that a good tenant looks after your investment as if it were their own. That is a Scriptural premise if anyone is interested.

The Reason I Don't Have the Rent Is:

Sometimes they try to get credit for good intentions.

1. I was going to mow the lawn, but my dad's lawnmower is broken.
2. I left a check at the house all week, but you never came by.
3. **The Question:**

"Why did you let the water run off the roof until there was a lake in the back yard and not call me?"

The Answer:

"I don't have a phone."

The Next Question:

"Why didn't you borrow a neighbor's phone."

The Answer:

"They won't let me use the phone."

The Next Question:

"Why didn't you write me a letter? I would have gotten it in one day."

The Answer:

"I can't read or write."

THE RENTAL ROLLER COASTER

***

I had a tenant who said that her husband had left her. She said that her uncle in another state was going to pay her rent and he would be calling me. He did, in fact, call me. He promised to send the check out in the next day's mail. He lived in a small town and had to go to town to get a money order. I told him I would give him 5 days. This was about 2003. At the end of five days, I called him, and he had another excuse. I did not fall for that a second time. In retrospect, I should have demanded that he wire me the money. Since I was not familiar with that type of money transfer, I lost several days' rent. Lesson learned.

Chapter 5

Unintended Consequences

If there is a problem with a house, I discuss it with the tenant before the move in, though they sometimes forget this conversation when they later want some changes made. I explained to one tenant that the covered patio roof was leaking and that I would either repair or tear it down but not at the time of her moving in. She rented it "as is." When the first rain came, and it started leaking she wanted it fixed immediately. I tore it down due to structural problems. She then wrote me a letter complaining that if she had known what I was going to do, she would not have said anything. That is called unintended consequences.

***

When someone calls about a rental and wants to know if I take pets, I tell them I might if I can see where the pet lives now. This filters out quite a few prospects. If someone tells me that the puppy is house-trained, I usually think that it translates into this: they have trained the puppy on someone's carpet and now they need a clean house. I tend to be suspicious.

***

If you allow tenants to have animals, be prepared to be held liable if the dogs do any damage, including biting someone. That being said, I have on occasion had a discussion with tenants involving liability insurance. When I see dangerous dogs tied with logging chains to heavy posts or cross ties, I assume this is not a family pet.

I do not intentionally rent to people with dangerous dogs, but the dogs sometimes show up after I have rented the house. I then insist that the tenant carry a three hundred- thousand-dollar liability insurance policy. Each time I have one of these conversations, the tenant has moved rather than pay for it.

***

Here is something that maybe should have been in the legal issues chapter, but these stories sometimes blur the lines so here it is. A woman applied to rent a three-bedroom house. After the usual question and answer session, we came to an agreement. THEN she said, "My son has a therapy dog. He doesn't function well without him. I have a letter from the doctor." I pondered this for a moment. I had already agreed to rent it to her. She would now have grounds for a discrimination lawsuit if I refused. I relented and said that she could have a dog.

At that point, I wasn't sure if I could charge a pet damage fee. I assumed not because the dog was a "therapy dog." She then said that they also had a bird because the therapist said he needed the bird too. I was getting suspicious but by then it was the "In for a dollar, in for a dime," kind of thing. I agreed to that, then she said the damaged boy had a snake. I balked at that and she said that she would get rid of the snake. When I later asked about it she said that the kids were very sad but that they had turned the snake loose in an adjoining field. So sad. :(

***

Speaking of dogs: There seems to be a lot of people who believe that Chihuahuas will keep children from getting asthma. Don't ask me, I don't understand it either.

***

I will sometimes drive by the house where the prospective tenant says that they live. One landlord in my support group calls on them with the excuse that they forgot to sign something. He also looks at the inside of their car. Untidiness, he believes, equates to a dirty house. He has been fooled by this when a tenant borrows a clean, late model car to apply for a rental. Checkmate occurs when the car they are driving is not the car they listed on the Rentals Application.

***

I had one tenant who rented a cinder block house. All the pipes were in between the double walls of cinder block in the center of the house. The pipes then exited the building. On a very cold day she called to tell me that the kitchen sink would not drain. I was not able to clean it out after what seemed an interminable amount of time on my knees, so I called my plumber. I call him mine only because I have spent an inordinate amount of money on his support.

I watched as he took off the p-trap and removed as much pipe as he could. He then attempted to snake the line. It did not work. He then took an extra-long screwdriver and he and I were both surprised as he chipped away at the congealed, frozen grease inside the line. In total, there was about six inches of grease that had built up in the line. There was enough grease in there to fry a chicken, which she may have done. I told the tenant to watch carefully because the next time this happened, she would have to do it herself.

***

Sue Happy Sara learned about unintended consequences the hard way. I gave her a Three Day Notice of Failure to Pay Rent. It stated that she now owed the rent plus a late fee. She was late with the rent and apparently thought that she could intimidate me by giving me a certified letter with demands for alterations to the house, citing her children's illnesses as the basis for the demands.

This letter included a demand that I recarpet the house, install new weather stripping on all the windows, replace the screen door, repair the bathroom sink and toilet, and fix the leak in the backyard.

By way of explanation let me say that I never rent a house until I have made it ready to move in because I don't want to work in a house with someone living there.

Someone had flushed a toy down the toilet, the screen door needed a screw tightened, and the water in the backyard was the result of someone using a post-hole digger while building a dog run, thus chipping the water line. Evidence of this was the digger leaning against the house.

I fired back a certified letter telling her when and how I would fix the things that I needed to fix and offering to let her out of the item of the contract which required a thirty-day notice before vacating the rental. I also expressed concern for the health of her children and suggested that they find a house that suited them as quickly as possible.

I soon received an invective-laced phone call from the grandmother. I tried to explain to the grandmother of the supposedly sick children that since my house was being blamed for the multiple illnesses of the children, I did not want to hinder them in any way from seeking a healthier environment. I suggested that they move at their earliest convenience. She continued ranting and threatening until I hung up. The woman either did not understand the content of my letter or was being deliberately obtuse. Sometimes it is hard to tell the difference.

I filed a Three Day Notice for Nonpayment of Rent and in ten days we were in court. You should know that in New Mexico, at least, only the Judge can "evict" a tenant. Don't ever state, in front of a Judge, that you have posted an eviction notice. They take umbrage at that. I made that mistake just once and was told, "Nobody evicts but me!"

The Magistrate judge ruled in my favor, sort of, and she was ordered to pay court costs in the amount of one hundred and two dollars. She was not required to pay the late fee. She had already moved out.

A postscript to this story is in order here. Sue Happy Sara then paid one hundred and seventeen dollars to file in District Court, appealing the verdict of the lower court, which was in the amount of one hundred and two dollars. This was a Court fee, not my late fee. As I write this, I can't remember her ever paying the court-ordered settlement.

I called my attorney, because a person should have one in District Court due to the procedures being more formal. After listening to my presentation of the facts, he said, "You don't have to worry. You have done as good a job as I could with the presentation and the judge is going to be fuming under his robes when he hears this case.

She told her story in court and waved a stack of medical bills, claiming that they were the result of living in my house for several months. I pointed out that she had six dogs, and she was allowed to have two. I had photographs to support my claim. The judge remarked that it could possibly be the six dogs running in and out of the house that had caused her children's allergies.

After the District Court Judge heard all of the evidence on both sides, he upheld the Lower Court verdict. It cost me an attorney consultation to be vindicated. I don't know what possessed her to tell the judge the following, as part of her argument.

She told the District Court Judge that she had mental problems. Was this an insanity plea? I don't know. I also don't know which planet she came from. Maybe the undiscovered planet of Bat Crap Crazy. It seems to have a lot of inhabitants.

Postscript: As it turned out, I got a call from the Welfare Fraud Department and I was able to give them useful information that the tenant revealed in court, under oath, which supported a case of welfare fraud against her.

It still cost me to go to the District Court. That is what attorneys are for. I just wrote it off my income tax and tried to forget about it. It's the time and wear and tear on my nerves that I couldn't write off.

***

Threatening to raise the rent (this can only happen after the end of the original contract) will sometimes inspire the tenant to take care of the yard, alley, greenery etc. I told one tenant that if she did not water the lawns and trees I would raise the rent by one hundred dollars and send someone to water the yards and mow. She started doing what she was required to do by contract. It is like raising a child. I repeat. There have to be consequences.

***

That said, some tenants absolutely will not put out mouse traps or poison, nor will they spray. They will, however, leave food on the counters, dirty dishes in the sink, a greasy stove, stacks of newspaper and brown paper bags (cockroaches love the glue in them.) When the house is over-run, they will then expect you to fix the problem by hiring a professional bug and varmint removal person. I refuse to do that. By this point, there are usually other issues of neglect, and I file the Seven Day Notice.

***

Look over the application closely. Some tenants have a reach that exceeds their grasp. Common sense should tell them whether they have enough income to pay the rent, car payment, utilities, insurance, and such things as food and car fuel. They may very well try to get into your house and then worry about whether they can make the rent

every month. Make sure they know that they should have renters' insurance. Most do not.

Chapter 6

Legal Issues

You and you alone have the legal responsibility to make sure that everything is kept on the legal side of things. If you don't, eventually this will come up, usually in a court of law. Not being vigilant will come back to bite you.

***

Once you have rented the house, you should call the utility companies and make sure they have been put in the tenant's name. Some of them will ride as far as they can on the credit of someone else.

***

One recent case came to light. I asked the tenant who Sucker Sally was, and the tenant said that she was a friend. A case of fraud was later filed against her by Sucker Sally. Here is that story.

Within a month of renting a house, I got a call from the power company and was told that there was a fraud case being developed against the tenant. She had used someone's identity to have the electricity turned on. This might not have seemed to be my problem but there are a few things wrong with this line of thought.

1. If the power is turned off, and then turned back on without the utility box being turned off, there could be a power surge which could ruin your heater, air conditioner, refrigerator, stove, microwave, or ice maker.

2. If the power is off for a length of time, the power company can require an electrical upgrade of the house. This could cost several thousand dollars.

3. If the house gets a bad reputation for not making payments on time, the power company may lock the box, causing the next tenant to pay a higher-than-normal deposit.

**

Always keep copies of everything. Eventually you will need it. Put notes in the file for each unit, noting anything that happens with the tenant, house and neighborhood. Eventually you will need this. It will also help to refresh your memory when you go to court. Notice I said when.

**

Get a copy of every police report. It gives you evidence and also makes sure that your tenant follows through with prosecution. Let me tell you a story about this: I will call them Latifa, Bubba, and Bubba's ex-wife, Rowena. He cold cocked her. But wait! It started like this:

One time I checked on the house and found a broken window. Latifa explained that Rowena had broken it because Bubba would not go outside to talk with her. Bubba had been living with Rowena prior to marrying Latifa. I told Latifa that if it happened again, she was to make a police report and that if she did not, I would evict her and Bubba.

I also told her to fix the window. Of course, they could not fix it because neither of them knew how to measure. When I found this out, I measured it for her, and they purchased and installed the glass. Not very expertly, but it kept out the wind.

Again, I went by and checked the house. I saw what appeared to be a pile of clothes under a tree, with a bicycle leaning up against the house. A closer inspection revealed that a skinny, bald-headed woman was sleeping soundly under the tree. I let the sleeping woman lie. I did, however, call the police and talk to the day commander.

I explained what the problem was and that I wanted to teach her a lesson by filing a criminal damage report. He laughed and said that he doubted that I could teach her anything because she had a rap sheet several pages long.

Another check of the house revealed another broken window. I knocked on the door and Latifa explained that Rowena had broken it again because Bubba wouldn't come out and talk to her.

I asked her if she filed a police report and she said,

"No."

"I told you to file a report or I would evict you. Why didn't you do it?"

"Because Bubba knocked her out."

After hearing the entire story I realized that we would have to wait until next time.

Rowena had tried to get Bubba's attention. She wanted him to come out and talk to her. He refused. She then hurled a rock through the window. Bubba came out of the house and cold cocked her. She lay there in the driveway until she regained consciousness. When she came to, she rode off on her bicycle.

Postscript to this story: Bubba finally moved out of Latifa's house and moved in with another woman. Thereafter, Rowena left Latifa alone.

***

Before you ever have to go to court it would be a good idea to sit in court and hear the proceedings. Some judges like to hear every little bit of information from both sides, some only want you to give the bare facts and then will ask you pertinent questions. Knowing this ahead of time will give you a chance to formulate your case in a manner that appeals to the judge.

Keep in mind that Magistrate and Municipal judges are appointed to fill seats, or they get elected. Neither one guarantees that they know very much about the law. They get sent to a few classes and then get on-the-job training. Sometimes this will be on your case. Some of them are former law officers of one stripe or another. Be advised that judges sometimes rule in a way that hurts everyone a little so that everyone wins. Here is what I think.

The reason that Solomon (of Bible fame) decided to cut the baby in half was not to hurt everyone a little. It was because he knew that the real mother would rather give up her child than harm it. I am not sure that judges understand this. In each case when I have been in a legal, binding contract, and they have chosen not to enforce it, they seem to have chosen instead to "split the difference."

They appear to use financial hardship as an excuse to put part of the burden on my shoulders. When I first got into this business, I thought that a judge's duty was to enforce a legally binding contract. I was wrong. Leviticus 19:15 says: "You shall do no injustice in court. You shall not be partial to the poor or defer to the great, but in righteousness shall you judge your neighbor." ESV. That is what I think.

***

A lawyer gave me some good advice one time. He gestured to his head and said, "Think with this." Then he gestured to his heart and said, "Feel with this. Don't get them confused." I did that one time and it cost me about twelve hundred dollars. This advice was part of his consultation fee. Here is the story:

I came across a woman who was living in a hovel and made arrangements to move her into one of my houses. I gave her fabric and instructions so she could make purses and sell them. I gave her other things to lift her spirits and finances. After a few months, she decided to move but left some things in the house for another month. Therefore, I was out two months' rent.

I took legal action to get her out. She got a free government attorney who sued me, claiming that I was holding some valuable antiques. I guess twenty-five pairs of tube socks, a broken dresser, and a broken washing machine full of stinking water constituted antiques. I ended up paying her five hundred dollars, and of course, my attorney fees. He said that it would be cheaper to pay her than for him to go to court and prove she was wrong. Boy did that rankle! Another lesson learned.

***

You will hear the saddest tales and your heart will tell you that it is in your power to fix it. You may feel magnanimous and sure that the Lord will shine down and bless you for your kindness. I will tell you this. Ninety-nine times out of one hundred you will get played. Tenants know how to work you, what to say, where and when to say it. People whom you help will frequently turn on you. They will not hesitate to lie in court. Judges sometimes cannot tell who is telling the truth. Sad to say.

***

New Mexico has a set of laws called the New Mexico Uniform Owner-Resident Relation Act. Check with your state laws and study them. When you think you know them, study them again. These are posted online and when I have a question, I look for updates. In New Mexico, there is a Landlord/Tenant Hot Line. The advice is free to tenants who claim to be low income, but the landlords have to pay. That gives you an idea of which way the government leans in this state. I am sure that each state has something comparable.

***

I had the opportunity to ask the assistant to the Governor if I could send him pictures of some of my houses, to see if some laws could be changed to be more equitable to the property owners. He said that it had been tried before but that "the lawmakers say that we are trying to pick on the poor people." And so goes the nation.

***

In this state, the landlord is responsible for rodent and insect control if the property is a multiple-housing unit but not if it is a single-family dwelling. Use your own best judgment. It is your house and if the situation gets out of control it may take several treatments to get it under control. By then the tenant has usually moved. I have never understood why some people will live with mice and cockroaches crawling around instead of using some form of control or even keeping the unit clean. Nasty. Nasty.

***

I guess I could inject here that the reason that I have never purchased multiple unit housing instead of single-unit houses is because I worked and people who rent apartments, at least in this small town, tend to move more than people who rent houses. Also, people who rent usually have children in school and there also seems to be more friction between neighbors in apartments. I don't like to referee.

I got called to the middle of one altercation. I owned two houses directly across the street from each other. The new tenant backed his trailer out of the driveway and hit the other tenant's car, which was parked on the street. Who got called? Of course!

Apparently, because I owned both houses, I was supposed to negotiate a settlement between them. I did not. I told them to report it to the police.

***

Officers can enforce any part of a criminal law, but they are not supposed to get involved in civil law. That could get you in trouble if you stand up for your rights. They have very wide discretion. On that note, this next story is best told as a play because of all of the actors involved.

Lolli's Story

I have changed the names in order to protect the guilty, the innocent, and the vindictive.

Here are the players in this little episode:

Lolli- The Little Old Landlady

CPO- City Police Officer

DT- Dying Tenant

CC- Coward of the County, a friend of DT.

CC called Lolli and said that DT was dying and that he (CC), and DT's daughters were cleaning out DT's house. DT was in the hospital and not expected to live. CC called Lolli after he and DT's girlfriend had removed most of the valuable things.

When Lolli arrived at the house, she noticed that the den, which had been converted into a workroom, was devoid of all tools. The external electrical system and workbench, which DT had installed, had been ripped from the walls. All the kitchen cupboards had been emptied and the kitchen appliances were missing, as was some of the furniture. All of the closets were empty.

DT's girlfriend and CC were loading things into their cars and claiming rights to things in the house. CC offered to sell some of the furniture to Lolli and she refused, stating that DT already owed her a month's rent and from the looks of the house, several thousand dollars in damages.

Then CC offered her a few things in return for the past due rent. Lolli accepted and wrote a letter stating the agreement. She also asked that an inventory be made of everything that had been or was being removed from the premises.

This is a legal requirement in New Mexico and required of all landlords. This was not done. CC was overheard instructing the movers to deliver some items to a third party. DT's daughters told Lolli that CC had the authority to store or dispose of everything in the house. CC and DT's girlfriend promised to leave the house ready for the next tenant to rent by the first of the month. This did not happen.

DT did not die. Several weeks after he got out of the hospital, he started going through <u>one</u> of his storage units. When he could not find some kitchen appliances and other things, he confronted CC.

CC, coward that he is, said that Lolli must have taken them. DT then went to the Police Department. DT complained to CPO, who is the city police officer, in case you are having trouble keeping track of the players in this little drama. CPO called Lolli, threatening her, refusing to identify himself by first name or badge number (three times), and refusing to listen to any explanation of the situation and the laws that apply. This was a civil matter, not criminal. CPO hung up on Lolli.

An hour later someone from the Sheriff's Office called Lolli and she explained everything to the deputy. He replied that he figured it was something like that and thanked her for her time. She thought that was the end of the situation.

She wrote a letter of complaint to the mayor about the unprofessional conduct, lack of knowledge of Landlord/ Tenant law and the failure of CPO to identify himself by first name or badge number.

Six weeks later CPO showed up at Lolli's house with three other officers, called Lolli, and said, "You need to get to your house. Right Now! I have a warrant for your arrest. If you do not get up here immediately, I will kick in the door!" Lolli told him that he better not damage her house. CPO then called a locksmith.

When CPO called Lolli and ordered her to get to her house because he had an arrest warrant, she showed up at her house and was arrested for fourth-degree larceny and taken to jail to be booked and released on her own recognizance. She subsequently visited her attorney, and it was explained to her that the value of items contested had to be above five hundred dollars for a charge of Fourth Degree Larceny.

Although DT placed a value of four hundred and seventy-five dollars on the contested items, the District Attorney's office agreed to prosecute for 4th degree larceny which is a charge of more than five hundred but less than twenty-five hundred and one dollar. Did you catch that?

SOOOO—-CPO had now involved a judge, four law officers, four squad cars, a locksmith, the District Attorney's office, and court personnel, for an illegal arrest.

Lolli's attorney cleared her name. She could have received eighteen months in jail and a five thousand dollar fine, had she been prosecuted as charged. No doubt the mayor had passed the letter to CPO's superior, the Chief of Police. CPO, while seething in court about the outcome of the case, at least had the satisfaction of paying Lolli back for the letter that she had written to the mayor. Such a letter would be entered into CPO's employment record, thus putting a black mark in his personnel file. No wonder he arrested Lolli.

Postscript to this: Lolli later had a friend check to see what the outcome was for the law officer. Apparently, he was put on suspension and quit the force, moving out of state.

***

It is always best to have an attorney draw up your rental agreements or leases. If you are landlording on a shoestring, get hold of two or three contracts that are being used in town. Compare them. You can also go online and download one, but keep in mind that some things might not apply in your state, or they may be outdated. Read the Owner-Resident Act and draw it up if you feel confident. You will find out soon enough if it is tight or full of holes.

***

I have been going to court for about eighteen years, but I still get sick to my stomach and have a hard time breathing when I walk into the courthouse. Be prepared to have your reputation slandered. Be prepared to be accused of all kinds of dastardly things. Don't get into arguments or try to defend yourself unless you feel very strongly about these things. Just keep in mind that the judge doesn't think any more of you or believe you any more than he does the biggest liar in the courtroom.

Also remember that while you may be familiar with the case and know all the little bits of information, the judge knows nothing. Be sure that you clarify everything. He will ask you to state your case. As the Plaintiff you will speak first. Do this thoroughly but succinctly. Practice before you go to court. Go over your notes beforehand so that you will show confidence in the rightness of your case. Judges don't care about your motives or anything that might have been said or promised by the tenant.

***

Never give a prospective tenant the house keys until sufficient money has changed hands. If they get in and don't pay, they can always claim that you gave them a key. That is why, if I think I might have a good, prospective tenant, I make them pay the deposit and put in the contract how long they have to pay the rent. That way, if they do not comply, I can evict them for nonpayment of rent.

I also have a clause in my contract that if they do not stay at least six months, I do not return the deposit. I make sure they understand this before I let them sign the contract. A judge might not support this since it is supposed to be a damage deposit.

Nevertheless... :)

***

Beware of accepting partial payments. If you do, it becomes a debt for which they cannot be evicted. One way I have handled this is by accepting the partial payment, putting it in an envelope, and labeling it. I tell the tenant that if I have to go to court I will bring the envelope. I have them sign the sealed envelope, across the flap. Never convert what they give you. Do not cash it, sign it or deposit it.

***

A Seven Day Notice of Noncompliance can be used if the tenant does not perform any item in the contract other than failure to pay rent. Once this is posted (with a date and time), they will have seven days to correct the deficiency. There is a place on the one I use that states whether this is the first or second warning within six months. If it is the second, you can file for an eviction. These things may have changed since I have had the opportunity to use them. Be sure to check everything I have stated. The laws may have changed!!! Also, the service procedures may have changed.

***

One such case arose when I tried to evict a tenant whose mother had attacked me and whose children had stopped up the plumbing with their toys and were damaging the house. Although the judge said that he was ruling in my favor, in fact, that was not so. He canceled the agreement. That was in my favor.

THEN -He failed to issue an eviction to the tenant. Therefore, I was in the untenable situation of having a squatter in my house. I can only surmise why he did this. She refused to leave and said that she had been told that she did not have to by a Legal Aid attorney. That is a government attorney who provides reduced or free legal assistance for poor people. Not for landlords. Legal Aid told the judge that they were trying to find her a house.

There were two ways of resolving this. One was to appeal it to the next higher court. This could have taken weeks. The next was to wait until the rent was not paid and then take her back to Magistrate Court. That is what I did, requesting another judge. He gave her three days to get out.

I will tell you that by the time I got her out, she had pulled up the carpet to form a pool to keep the sewage from coming any farther into the house than the master bedroom. I had to cut the soggy, stinking carpet into small enough strips that I could drag it through the house to the dumpster. I then had to cut the wet sheet rock out and tear out the disgusting baseboards. I couldn't ask anyone to help due to the health issues involved.

I was so furious that I wanted to take a piece of the stinking, filthy carpet and deposit it on the desk of the Legal Aid person. They don't have to deal with the repercussions of their actions. Again- Discretion is the better part of valor.

***

I was once accused, from the witness stand, of kidnapping a tenant. She swore under oath that it was true. Here is the real story.

I was visiting with a neighbor when her cleaning lady showed up. I will refer to her as Troublemaker. She was crying and had bruises up and down her arms. She said that her alcoholic boyfriend kept telling her to get out of the house they shared and yet he demanded that she give him her paycheck.

We asked her if she wanted to leave, and she said yes. I offered to put her and her son in a vacant house if she would not tell her boyfriend where she went. She promised. We then made a plan for the following day. The neighbor and I would each take a flatbed trailer with our pickups, and I would also bring one young man to help load the furniture. She said that her son would also help.

The boyfriend showed up while we were there and threatened Troublemaker, choking her. I immediately called the Police Department and Boyfriend lunged at me in a threatening manner. I said, "Go ahead. I have the Police on the line." When the police showed up, he was arrested for domestic violence. We continued packing and got her moved. One thing we found was a three-foot lead pipe, filled with something, hidden behind a chair. We took that too.

When I was on the witness stand to testify at Boyfriend's trial, I was accused of tax evasion, having an affair with the twenty-year-old son of Troublemaker, (I was nearly seventy at the time), and the aforementioned kidnapping. My neighbor was accused of the same. The boyfriend got off with probation. Troublemaker went back to him. Her son went to jail for the auto theft. You just can't help some people.

***

I had a tenant who was on HUD. I named her Mack as in Mack The Knife. She was in violation of her Lease Agreement because she did not have the electricity or gas turned on. When CYFD called on her to check on the children's welfare, the inspector did not notice that the family was eating sandwiches in the dark. I called and reported this to the agency. I don't know if they did anything about it.

We have a legal responsibility to report child or elder abuse. Even if we did not, I believe we all have a moral responsibility.

These tenants apparently did not want me around (they owed me rent), so when the sewer line backed up, they took the cap off the sewer cleanout, letting the sewage run out onto the ground. They stacked empty boxes and broken furniture around the pool of sewage so I would not notice. I filed a Notice Of Failure To Pay Rent.

I did a drive-by on the morning we were due in court. Mack was in jail for stabbing her husband, so her mother showed up. She had called Code Enforcement that morning and reported that I refused to fix the sewer line. She then reported this to the judge. He asked me if I knew about this, and I replied that I had driven by that morning and saw boxes and furniture piled over the cleanout. He dismissed her charge against me.

Later, when I got the house back, I found that the reason the sewer backed up was because the children had dropped water balloons down one of the cleanouts, effectively

blocking them from flowing properly. This house had two cleanouts because the bathrooms were on the opposite ends of the house.

Since Mack had gone to jail for stabbing her husband, I let the grandmother stay in the house to care for the children. When she did not pay the rent as agreed and I attempted to get her out, the deputy would not enforce the eviction notice from the court because Mack was in jail, not in the house, and there were three minors in the house. I had to file in court against the grandmother to get the eviction. By that time Mack, her husband, the grandmother, and three children were all living in the house.

Prior to this, the water department had sent me a letter threatening to tear up my water lines if I did not take action against the tenant. The Water Department had turned off the water. The tenant turned it back on. The Water Department then slugged the line. The tenant managed to bypass the plug. The utility then removed the meter. Next, the tenant ran a line from a neighbor's property. This is illegal.

Rather than contest the proposed action of the Water Department, I responded to the letter by calling and explaining my legal problems. I assured the Water Department that I was actively involved in getting the deadbeats out of my house. I don't take kindly to being threatened but I did understand their dilemma. I just did not like them thrusting their problem on me or threatening me. Sometimes it is easier to go with the flow than stand your ground on things like this. Choose which hill you want to defend. I was going to have to resolve this issue regardless.

***

When I receive a damage deposit, the judges I have gone before won't let me use it for unpaid rent, even though it is stated in the contract, which the tenant signs. They will, however, consider the deposit in making a judgment on how much the tenant owes me.

It is my understanding that it is supposed to require another court hearing to determine the distribution of the money. I have had judges specifically tell the deadbeat tenants, <u>from the bench</u>, that they can sue me if I don't comply. I even had a judge give legal advice, <u>from the bench</u>, on a case on which he had just ruled! And yet, when I tried to ask for a clarification, he held up his hand and said, "This case is over!" Is that fair and impartial? I have always been very careful to adhere to the Landlord/Tenant Relations Act.

***

When the tenant does not pay the past due rent and damages the house, it necessitates another Court action (which you will have to pay for.) By the time you get back in court, the tenant is long gone and there is no way to track them down. Our taxes pay for this inefficiency. Talk about blind justice!

***

Keep a camera with you at all times. Or have a good picture-taking phone. Judges like pictures. I wish somebody would invent one with scratch-and-sniff photos.

***

If you require paperwork in addition to a filled out application, be sure to use a recognized consumer agency. If you deny tenancy because of anything else, you are liable to legal action. You could end up in trouble with the Federal Trade Commission or some other Federal Agency.

***

If there is an emergency in the house, such as a lack of water, you are required to provide alternate housing while the situation is rectified. One fine spring day the temperature turned hot while I was out of town. I was about two hours away, and on my way back home, when a tenant asked her neighbor to go into the attic and take the cookie sheet off of the evaporative cooler.

This is a metal sheet that is in place during the winter to prevent cold air from blowing into the air ducts when the heat is turned on. He stepped on the water line and flooded the house. I had to provide her with a motel room while I had it fixed. Legal responsibility is hard to prove and if the tenant has no money, what difference does it make? I ignored her when she complained about the damage to her stored possessions.

***

Sometimes checking social media such as Facebook will reveal enough to help you make a decision regarding a tenant.

***

One tenant dropped his insurance because he had wrecked one side of his pickup in a DUI accident. He had his name tattooed on his forehead. I can't tell you what it is, so how about Tattoo? When a branch from a recently trimmed tree fell on his vehicle during a heavy windstorm, Tattoo threatened me with legal action if I did not reimburse him for the damage. The teenage son made the remark, "Now we own your pickup." I told him to not even start with that BS. Nothing came of the threats, but it was unpleasant and unnecessary.

***

If a tenant makes a threat to you, be sure to get it on record. If the police won't make a report, call or write the tenant's parole officer, case worker, etc. After you have done that, put a note in the house file. You may need proof of a pattern of threatened violence. Keep in mind that most of them are just mouthing off. If they do anything, it will be to throw a rock through a window or slash your tires. Both of these things have happened to me.

***

You can hardly get a deposit large enough to cover the damages that can be caused by a tenant. In New Mexico, if you hold a deposit larger than the rent, you have to keep it in a separate account and pay interest on it. By the time you have paid someone to rake up the yard, reseed and water and or replace the lawn, haul dirt to fill the holes, repair the fences, clean and repair the house you will be out quite a bit of money, even if you do a lot of it yourself.

Does this still sound like a viable option to you? It is not for the faint of heart or stomach. But be of good cheer. You can write it off of your income tax. :)

***

This brings to mind a strange incident. It is the only time that a tenant or their family member has laid a hand on me.

I rented to a woman with five children. Let's call her Vaguely. I felt sorry for her because she did not seem to be holding a full deck of cards. She had a boyfriend. She also had a mother. Let's call Mother—The Witch. The reason will soon be evident. I had received a letter from HUD, stating that the house that I had rented to Vaguely was due for an inspection. This happens periodically. Sometimes every few months, sometimes once a year. I could write a small book about that subject alone.

Anyway- An inspection of the house revealed some things that would not pass. The reasons were all because of tenant damage. Missing kitchen cabinet door, missing caulk from around the bathtub, et cetera ad nauseam. I scolded the tenant and told her I was going to Home Depot to pick up what I needed to do the repairs. While I was there, I received a call from The Witch saying that the police were there and I was in trouble and better get to the house.

I left my basket at the counter and went immediately to the house. The Witch, Vaguely, and Vaguely's boyfriend were the only ones there. Looking back, I realize that I really walked into that one. If the cops (constable on patrol) wanted to talk to me, they would have called me. DUH!

After an unpleasant interaction with The Witch, I got my camera and started taking pictures of the damage. I was in the bathroom taking pictures of the caulking, which had been removed from around the tub and thrown in the trash. The Witch tried to grab it from me, and I held it away from her. She continued to verbally assault me and pushed me.

I had a split second to decide whether to take the high road or give her a swift uppercut to the chin. In that period of time, I noticed her shiny white false teeth and knew that if I hit her, I would, at the very least, break those store-bought teeth. I chose to walk away. We were in a very small bathroom. As I stepped out the door, The Witch gave me a shove. I kept walking and went to the kitchen and grabbed my ladder.

By that time, The Witch, Vaguely and Boyfriend were advancing on me. I held the ladder between them and me as I called the police. I then went outside to wait beside my pickup.

When two police cars showed up, one officer interviewed me and the other officer took The Witch to the far side of the yard and stood, with feet spread, guarding her. The first officer then began talking to the tenant. When he was finished with her, he sent her across the street to wait.

Before very long The Witch started chanting in a strange language and bowing east, west, north and south. The lead officer then asked "Officer Regalado, (not his real name) is everything alright over there?" Officer Regalado turned slowly around, trying to keep a smile off his face. He said, "Yes sir, everything is just fine." Behind him The Witch continued with her bowing and incantations. I had the distinct impression that she was trying to put a curse on me. Maybe the officers did too.

The lead officer said that he would stay while I did whatever I needed to do. I told him that I was not going to fix anything, I was going to file for an eviction.

***

You have to give twenty-four hours' notice before entering a house once it is rented. If the tenant is reluctant to let you in, it is not a good sign. Be prepared. He or she may be hiding something. Repairs must be done in a timely fashion. This is usually one week, except in case of emergency. If there is an emergency that can't be fixed in a day, you may be responsible for providing the family with housing. This usually means a motel room.

***

I had one tenant call me while I was out of town for Thanksgiving. He said that the drains had slowed down on Wednesday, but he was working and did not want to deal with it, so he waited until Friday. I called around and no plumber was working on the day after Thanksgiving. I told him to get a motel room and I would have it taken care of on Monday. That cost me several hundred dollars. No judge was going to take my side on that. Some things you just know. It turned out that he did not run hot water down the kitchen drain and it got clogged with the normal crud that gets in kitchen pipes.

***

This same tenant later moved out. When he called to ask if he could take his security system, I said yes. My painter had already painted the room when the tenant returned and cut a hole in the wall and tore out the wiring. It did not occur to me that he would not unscrew the box and disconnect the wires. This sort of thing may explain why I have high blood pressure.

***

Regarding damage- There is an item called normal wear and tear. This is usually up to the discretion of the judge.

THE RENTAL ROLLER COASTER

***

By New Mexico state law, you have thirty days to send a letter with a settlement for damages. Frequently you will not have time to clean and repair the house and get all the bills paid before the thirty days have passed. Guesstimate the damages. You probably won't get reimbursed anyway, but you can try. If the music is playing, you have to dance.

***

Always take plenty of pictures before you begin to clean and repair. Witnesses are a good thing to have. This is where your support group comes in.

***

You are not allowed to change the locks until you have gained possession of the house unless you give the tenant a set of the new keys. Likewise, they are not allowed to change the locks without giving you a set of new keys. Don't count on this. A helpful hint: If you buy your locks from a hardware store or locksmith, they will usually charge a nominal fee to rekey them. This is cheaper than buying new locksets.

***

Always carry new lock sets to change the locks when the Sheriff calls you to take possession of the house after a court ordered eviction. You are required to show up when they call.

They will give the offending tenants anywhere from ten to thirty minutes to finish packing. Even though it has been several weeks since you filed and went to court- seven days that the judge gave them to vacate, and at least one or two days after you have gone back to the court, filed a Plea for Production, taken it to the Sheriff's Office, paid the service fee, then two to four more days after the sheriff's deputy warned them that they had two days to vacate.

It is not like the tenants are surprised by all of this. They know how to scam the system. I don't know if this is state law or just local procedure. The clock you hear ticking is the money you don't get.

***

Also, if a tenant moves out, I always change the locks. Sometimes I switch them from one house to another. It saves a little money and no one knows but me.

***

If you have to evict someone, be prepared for a filthy house and usually stopped up plumbing. Some people do not display much pride in their living conditions, even for health reasons. They can be vindictive and frequently put things down the drains. The water is frequently turned off for several days before they vacate so be prepared for a toilet full of ...You guessed it.

***

I know of one elderly landlord who had a trailer park in the county. He owned the trailers. He filed for an eviction and when the people left, he failed to immediately inspect the house. He was soon having complaints about plumbing backups in all the other trailers. It took him a while to trace down the problem.

The evicted tenants had left the hot water running in the trailer. This caused the water heater to run constantly, thus running up his electric bill and causing the septic tank, which served several units, to fill up. It was a very expensive proposition to have it pumped out and all of the stopped up sewer lines cleared. Plus the cleanup. People can be evil.

***

I have had deputies shove people off my property and block them from returning for their items. I had one occasion when the Sheriff's Department called me to meet them for an eviction. The tenant had parked at the front door and had just started to load their car. I went to the back door and started to replace the lock set.

The tenant warned me to be careful because his dog bites. That dog then got loose and the deputies drew their guns, ready to shoot the dog. The tenant then shouted that the dog was not vicious and pleaded with them not to shoot him.

Liar, liar, pants on fire. The people continued to load the vehicles after they had been told to leave the property. A deputy then ordered the car removed and shoved the man off the property. Yikes!

***

An inspection of another house resulted in my finding a drawing of a marijuana leaf taped to the son's bedroom door. I figured that he was a marijuana aficionado. I did not think a lot about it until I got an eviction order from the court and was able to begin the cleaning and repairs. I found pot growing in a storage room. I then removed the picture on the door and found that it was covering a large hole.

***

Speaking of holes. I had one couple move into a two bedroom house. She soon moved out. I offered the man a job to help him pay his rent. I bought him a cheap car and let him work off the debt. He bragged about being a big-time drug dealer in Seattle or somewhere. I did not believe him because he would say things like, "I would walk the street real cool like and then shake hands with someone. No one could tell that he gave me money and I gave him dope. Then I would take it to a man in a car who was waiting to take the money to the bank."

I have seen enough movies to know that the top dog does not get out and sell on the street and then send a runner to the bank with the money. I let him run his head. That is how I find out things. Just let them keep talking.

It wasn't long before I had occasion to approach his front door and saw what appeared to be a four-inch ax cut in the metal door, about head high. I asked him about it and he said that some people were trying to break in. Red flag! The metal door had also been bent. It must have been one heck of a fight! He had not reported it to me.

He soon got into drugs, (probably had been all along), sold the car, started breeding puppies in the house, and would not show up for work. I think the reason he left was to avoid the drug dealers who were no doubt looking for their money. I heard many stories over the next few months about his downward spiral.

I had to pull up the carpet, shampoo the wooden floors, and seal them with oil based Kilz before I could re-carpet. Oil based Kilz is your friend! A fight must have occurred by the front door because the entire frame of the door had been detached from the wall. The carpet no longer met the threshold. There was also what appeared to be a two-inch knife puncture near the bottom of the door.

I surmised that someone was on the floor, slashed out at someone, missed, and buried the knife in the door. But what do I know? I was able to straighten the door by holding a two-by-four at an angle at the top of the door and repeatedly bumping against the door until it would close properly.

***

Get a deposit for a garage door opener. If they take it with them, you will not only have to purchase another one but will also have to recode the box that operates the door. That is unless the unit is an old one, in which case you will have to purchase a new unit.

***

I carry an umbrella liability policy. Check with your insurance company. It may be worth your while to have all your properties in an LLC. Check with your attorney.

***

When you replace your refrigerators be very careful. Place the door against the wall until you can remove it from the property, or better yet, take the door off of it. I know of one couple who lost two boys this way. The children climbed into a refrigerator and were not found until it was too late. Not in one of my houses, but still. It was so sad. Did I mention drive-bys? Every evening after work I would drive by some or all my houses. Sometimes down the alley, sometimes on the street. You can often spot trouble before they get out of hand.

***

Be careful or you can be trapped in a discrimination lawsuit. Use caution and do not ask any questions which are unlawful and be sure to ask the same questions and ask for the same requirements from everyone you interview. If you feel that you have reason to ask for a police report or a credit report, be sure to require that of everyone. The reason this comes to mind is this: I had the occasion to help someone with his rentals.

Because of the history of the rentals, I required a police report from all applicants. One woman was indignant that I required this and was sure that I had singled her out. She left and within a matter of minutes, a man came racing up to the house and jumped out of his pickup. I was working on the front porch.

"Is this house for rent?"

"Yes, it is."

"I want to rent it."

"Don't you want to look inside, first?"

"No. What will it take to rent it?"

"You need to fill out the application and provide a police report."

He got in his truck and left. He apparently thought he could trap me. There will always be people who are landmines of trouble, hoping to sue. Be careful.

***

Renting to people who do not speak English can present problems. How will you collect the rent if they can't tell you when they will have it? How will they tell you if there is an emergency in the house? How will they tell you if they are moving? How can they understand the contract?

Would it even be legal if they don't know what they are signing? I make sure that each prospective tenant reads the entire contract in front of me before I let them sign. If they are not good readers, I explain each paragraph. I don't want anyone to have any misunderstanding of what I require.

***

One thing you can do is have a place to initial beside every item on your contract. It is my opinion that many a prospective tenant takes the contract home to sign because they can neither read nor write.

***

Each time I went to one house, the screen door was swinging freely in the wind. I told the tenant that if he wanted to keep the door on the house, to keep it latched. Another inspection revealed that the screen door had been damaged irreparably. I told the tenant that he was going to have to pay for it. He said that it was not his fault but the fault of his friends. I told him that he needed better friends, who would respect private property. He paid for it.

***

One tenant overflowed his washing machine and flooded the kitchen floor. As a result, the wooden subfloor floor warped, and the threshold of the back door swelled. Because the back door would not open, the tenant kicked the door open. Because I would not fix it until the wood had dried out, he called code enforcement and told the officer that his wife was afraid to be in the house because the door would not latch. He said that he moved the washing machine in front of the door for safety's sake.

I got a letter from the city and had to shave down the door before it was dry. I probably could have waited until I got a second notice, but I didn't. If I had, the floor would have had time to dry out. If a tenant wants to screw you over, there is very little you can do to stop it. All you can do is try to mitigate the damage.

***

I got a phone call from a tenant one time when I was out of state. It was a holiday. The tenant said that every time anyone touched the kitchen faucet, they got a shock. I immediately called my electrician and asked him to check it out for me. When he called me back, this is what he had found- There was a single light bulb on in the house. Nothing else would turn on.

Tracing down the problem, he found that someone had tried to pull down the wires going into the house from the power pole. They were hanging low, and someone had tried to separate the wire from the cable that stabilized it. The brass grounding rod was missing from the breaker box. This grounds the house to prevent electric shocks and fires. It also redirects excess current to the ground instead of appliances, for the most part. All of this required immediate action.

Fortunately for me, he was a very conscientious man. He immediately left to get the parts necessary and took the time to do everything necessary to make the house safe again. On a holiday. When I returned home, I threatened the tenant with eviction and tampering. If the city had found out about that, they might have made me rewire the house. That was a VERY stressful event for me.

***

Even Escrow Companies go sideways:

Here is a nerve-jangling, hair-raising incident that took several months to unravel. It seldom happens because of stiff regulations and government oversight, but it happened to me and many other Landlords in 2019.Technically this is not a Landlord problem but since these properties were rentals before I sold them on Real Estate contracts, I guess this qualifies to be put in this book.

I, along with over sixteen hundred other Landlords, had our Real Estate contracts managed by the only Escrow Company in town. The owner of the Company absconded (I should say allegedly) with the money from a trust account which was set up to hold all of the money set aside for the taxes and insurance on the various accounts. It amounted to about one and one-half million dollars. When the theft was discovered, the New Mexico Regulation and Licensing/Financial Services Division swept in, shut down the company and seized all of the files. They were transferred to the State office in Santa Fe.

This put everyone in a quandary. What to do? The Escrow Real Estate Contract states that no money is to be given to the seller and all payments must go through the Escrow Company. Another company was quickly set up and fast-tracked through the vetting process. This took a month or two. It took several months for the new company to process all of the contracts. As they processed each contract the buyers and sellers were required to go to the office and sign a new agreement.

The new Escrow Company sent out letters of request to each buyer with instructions that the request to the State for each contract be sent to the new Escrow Company and stating that we, the buyers and sellers, agreed to have them manage each account. These letters had to be signed by every owner and every buyer for each property. We then had to send the requests by certified mail to the State Inspectors and wait for the real estate contracts to be sent to the new Escrow Company.

In the meantime, my buyers needed to know what to do. As I stated somewhere in this book, I have always tried to conduct my business so I can explain it to a judge and to God.

I did not want my buyers to get behind in their payments, but I wasn't allowed to receive any money. What to do? I set up a separate trust account for all the payments. I then invited each buyer to come to my home and sit down while I tried to explain to them that their money had been stolen. Since this was November and the property taxes and property insurance premiums were due in December, they would have to come up with at least half of the property taxes and the yearly insurance in one month.

Some of my buyers did not speak very good English so it was hard to make them understand. Some of them said, "That's OK, I already paid each month." It was heartbreaking for me to watch them try to understand that someone had stolen their money.

I put every payment in the trust account and did not touch it. When we got it all sorted out, I turned over all the money to the new Escrow Company and they then gave me back my part of each payment. It was nearly a year before all of my contracts were processed.

Here are two cases that gave me a lot of trouble. The first was a contract that I had as the buyer. The sellers were a couple who lived in Alaska and then moved to the States. The Escrow Company did not have a current address because the payments were handled by a company that contracted to make sure that all of the taxes and insurance got paid. I tried to contact the man who handled this, but he had moved to another state. When I tracked him down, he said that he no longer did that for them.

I don't remember how I got hold of two phone numbers. One of them was disconnected and one did not answer. It was in Idaho or someplace like that. In a day or two I received a call from the seller. She was living in Texas. Apparently, I had left a message on the phone of the seller's son. I explained what had happened and what I needed from her. She seemed dubious. I gave her the case number so she could look it up.

She said that she was divorced. Her husband had moved to Japan and married again. The new couple was now living in India. In the end, he had to go to the US Embassy to get the papers notarized. He faxed them to his ex who then faxed them to me. It took quite a bit of explanation before the State would accept the facsimile of a facsimile instead of the real paperwork, but they finally did.

The second case involved a double-wrapped Real Estate Contract. I sold a house on a contract to a couple. They sold it on a wrap to another couple. That means that another couple signed a Real Estate Contract to buy the house from the first couple. The couple separated and the husband moved back to Mexico. There was a lot of wrangling to get him to sign the papers. My buyers wanted me to deal with the Feds, but I convinced them that I could not because I was not a party to their contract. Their buyer was behind on his payments, which meant that the first couple was behind in their payments to me. I could have taken ownership of the property because of the default. I decided to put the delinquent payments at the end of our contract and let them start fresh. I forgave all of the late fees. What a mess!

Chapter 7

Do You Swear To Tell the Truth

This chapter is about some of the legal pitfalls and incidents that I have encountered and things that may help you maneuver the minefield of legalese. I used to naively believe that a judge would enforce any legally binding contract signed by two consenting adults. Don't count on it.

***

In Chaves County, the judge has the discretion of giving the tenant three or seven days to vacate. He cannot give the tenant more than seven days. He will give them seven days. I started putting in my contracts that the tenant agrees that if I have to file for an eviction, he agrees to be out in three days. I had occasion to try this out in court. The judge said, "I am going to disallow that." Well! So much for enforcing a legal, binding contract.

***

One reason I mention this is because most people want to start the rent on the first of the month. By the time you get to court and then wait seven days for the eviction plus any additional time that it takes and then you clean it up, you have lost at least three weeks. That means that you have already lost a month of rent. If it is the middle of the month, I let the new tenant pay to the first, so everything gets lined out. If it is just a few days, I don't charge them. That makes them happy. Everyone likes free.

***

You will have to file a Writ of Restitution to remove a tenant. In Chaves County, in Twenty-fourteen, the cost is seventy- seven dollars. The tenant, however, can claim that he cannot afford to file against you, and he gets to file

62

for free. You are not allowed to serve a legal instrument of the Court on the tenant. You must select a court-appointed officer of the court (process server).

The clerk will ask you to select one from a list or you can designate one. At the present time (2015) that cost is about twenty-five dollars or forty-seven if you want to use the Sheriff's Department. Once you go to court, if you prevail, the tenant is then given an amount of time to get out. If they are not out, you then have to go back to the court and file a Plea for Production. This is the only thing that is free.

***

If you are able to rent the unit to another tenant before the vacating month is up, the judge will expect you to reduce the amount due by the former tenant. In fact, every judge I have gone before will only grant you the number of days that he expects the tenant to be in the house. Never mind that you have to go back to court to file a Plea for Production and then wait for the Sheriff to pick it up at the Court.

Some districts have a designated process server. Others just have an officer do the service when they have time. They will not attempt to serve the Plea for Production until you have paid forty-seven dollars to the dispatch officer on duty (2014 dollars.)

***

It will then take about two days for the process server from the Sheriff's Office, and there is only one in Chaves County, to give the tenant notice that he has 2 full days to get out. Then at the end of two full days, he will post a notice of eviction and give the tenant another two full days to remove his belongings. I don't know if this is a state law or just the procedure of the local office. The rules may change as each new High Sheriff comes into office.

The tenant is then allowed to take his things off of your property and put them in front of your property or in the alley or in the empty lot next door for as long as he wants or can get by with it. This can give him another week or so to remove his belongings.

***

I have had professional renters not bother to remove anything until the deputy gets there to put them out. The deputy will then give them as much as 30 minutes to finish loading their things. I usually speak up at this point to move things along.

When you are called and told that the deputy is going to the house to remove the tenant be sure to have new locks in your possession. The officer will expect you to change them while he is there. That way he knows that the house is secure when he leaves. Check the windows to be sure they are locked. The tenant will climb through the window at some other time to remove anything he has left behind. That includes your cleaning supplies or anything else you leave there. Again, block the doors or they may kick them in. I sure hate to fix a wooden door and frame on a cinder block house. You have no idea how difficult that is!

***

The things you should ask yourself before you file in court are:
1. Do I have the stomach for this?
2. Do I have the time?
3. Do I have the energy?
4. Do I have the mental strength?
5. Is it worth it financially?
6. And most important is- How much negativity can I stand in my life?

Many experienced landlords say NO to those things and just go about repairing their property and finding the next tenant. Onward and upward!

***

If you have an emergency. even one of the tenants making, such as a water pipe that was stepped on when they were in the attic, you are required by law to furnish the tenant with housing until you get things repaired. Yes, indeed!! Stupidity on their part_does_ become your emergency. For the sake of your house, peace of mind, and relationship with the tenant, just keep your mouth shut until you can speak in a calm and rational manner. I refer you to the end of this book for the Landlord's Prayer.

THE RENTAL ROLLER COASTER

***

The tenant is required to send a certified letter for anything except a dire emergency. They don't. They call and expect immediate action. Tell them what you are going to do and when. Then follow through with a letter, restating the conversation. Keep a copy. Eventually, you will need one of these in court.

***

One recent case came to light. I checked on the utility transfer and found that the power was in someone's name which I did not recognize. I asked the tenant who S. R. was, and she said that she was a friend. Within a month I got a call from the power company and was told that there was a fraud case being developed against the tenant. This might not seem to be my problem but there are several things wrong with this reasoning.

If the power is turned off and then on, it could damage the refrigerator, stove, heater, and air conditioning unit. Also, any appliances or television sets that may be in the house could be damaged. I lost a microwave and ice maker this way. If the house gets a bad reputation for payments, the power company may lock the box, causing future problems, especially for prospective tenants. The power company may require a large deposit from the next tenant. Your new tenant may begin to distrust you and the caliber of the neighborhood.

***

I was in court one time and the judge told the tenant and me to go out into the foyer and come to an agreement as to how the tenant was going to pay me. We both agreed to a repayment schedule. She signed a note with our handwritten agreement, I presented it to the judge, and he dismissed us. Do you think that she followed through? No, she disappeared. Of course, I never saw her again. One more case of social engineering gone awry.

She moved in with her daughter, who managed an apartment complex. Because she worked for her daughter, I filed a case with the property owner but was ignored.

A mediation group was set up after this. In order to ease some of the load of the judges, a committee of men agreed to hear grievances. I was ordered to do one of these for one case. I agreed to some concessions and so did the man I had a claim against. He then said to them, "Yes, I agree to all of this, but I am not going to pay her!"

If they can't get people to do the honorable thing or obey court-ordered actions, why would they keep their word to a group of volunteers, who have no authority? Any wonder that this effort soon folded?

***

One time I took up the carpet in a living room and bedroom and replaced it with hard flooring because of damage caused by the tenant. I charged the tenant for the least of the two rooms. The judge seemed impressed with my sense of fairness. I got the judgment for the damage. I did not get the money. I used to think I could teach honesty and civility.

***

I have had several cars abandoned when tenants move out. I have yet to find one that ran or had any value. I call a towing company to remove them. They always call the Police Department to see if it is stolen. One time the tow truck driver refused to pick up the car and the police showed up because it was stolen. I had to leave it in the driveway until they contacted the owner.

When he examined it and realized that everything of value had been removed, he did not want it back. Then I could have it towed. Gurgle, gurgle. That is money down the drain while you wait for the car to be towed, so you can rent the house. Are you on your lunch break or are you working on the weekend? Your time is never your own and you can't deduct it from your income tax.

If you meet the tow truck driver and sign a consent form, he will remove the vehicle. There is a way to keep the vehicle if you want it, but I don't think it is worth the trouble. Ask your local Department of Motor Vehicles or State Police for information about this.

***

Keep blank legal papers. Notice of Abandonment, Three Day Notice of Non-Payment, Seven Day Notice, Thirty Day Notice, Plea For Production, etc. It will save you time and gas going to the Court House. Just be sure that you have current forms in your master file. Also, keep EPA lead-based paint warning pamphlets in your file. You are required by law to give one of these to each tenant. Have them sign a paper saying that you gave them one or that they have one in their possession. I include that in the Rental Agreement.

***

If you dislike keeping records as much as I do, try this: Keep one file for each house. Put every receipt for that house in the file. Put the rental agreement, the application, insurance and any notes that you make concerning any happenings at the house. Include any notices and letters to and from you and police reports. It makes it easy when you get things ready to do your taxes or have them done. It will also keep everything in one place if you have to go to court. The notes, pictures and letters will refresh your memory.

Chapter 8

Collecting Rents

According to most financial institutions, and the government, a family should spend About twenty-eight percent of their income for lodging. Renters typically pay a lot more.

***

Determine where you are going to collect rent. I prefer to go to the rental unit. This gives me a chance to check the house and the tenants seem to be more chatty this way. I find out what is going on in their lives and maybe get a preview of what I can expect in the future such as job loss, divorce, medical conditions, etc.

***

I rented to a young man who had worked for me on my farm. I thought that our past association would preclude him from trying to scam me. His mother was also a friend of mine.

He moved into a three-bedroom house with his wife and two kids. Following my usual procedure, I left the water on with the understanding that they would put the water utility in their names within three days. This did not happen. I had made the choice to let the family move in and pay the rent in increments due to the wife starting a new job.

Then the excuses started. "My wife's employer withheld the first two weeks' pay."

"What about your paycheck?"

"My boss is out of town. He should be back on Wednesday. I will pay you when my wife gets paid."

On Wednesday he did not get his check. I waited until the two weeks had come and gone.

"Do you have the rent?"

"My wife had to buy a lift belt and uniforms for work."

"Why hasn't the water been put in your name?"

"I will do that tomorrow."

"When will you have the rent?"

"This Friday."

"I expect this to get done."

Next visit.

"Do you have the rent?"

"My wife had to take a class and she wasn't reimbursed for it."

On Saturday I went to the house to collect the rent. Although both cars were at the home and the two young children were playing on the sidewalk, no one answered my knock on the door.

I asked the children where their parents were. The oldest said that neither of them was at home. I did not believe them and since the children were ages eight and six, I could have called Children, Youth and Families. I did not make the call although it bothered me that children so young had been taught to lie. I posted a Three Day Notice of Non Payment of Rent.

The next day I knocked on the door. Again, no answer. I turned off the water at the meter. The next time I knocked on the door I did not receive an answer. The water had been turned on again. I called the Water Company and found that it was still in my name. I was extremely angry at this point because there were obvious signs that they were at home and now they were stealing water from me.

I looked for tape and could not find any in my truck. I found a nail but could find no hammer. I did, however, have the pipe wrench with which I had turned off the water.

In all fairness I should say that I probably would not have answered the door at this time either, not wanting to face a pipe wrench wielding, very angry landlord.

Because the last note was left nailed to the front door, after one week I posted an Abandoned Property Notice. I took a picture of the Abandoned Property Notice and at the end of seven days, I hired two people to go into the house with me and remove everything we could load. This included clothing, dishes, furniture and even the wet clothes in the washing machine.

About six weeks later I got a call from the wife, and she wanted to know where her things were. I told her that they were in storage. She asked how much she owed me. I told her four hundred and eighty-five dollars, for rent and storage fees. She whined, "But the rent is only three hundred and fifty."

I know," I replied, "It would have been cheaper to pay the rent, wouldn't it?"

The wife then said that she had talked to a realtor and that I could not keep her things and she was going to sue me. I countered with, "I wouldn't take legal advice from a realtor. You should consult an attorney. You might mention to him that I have a police report showing that drug paraphernalia was found in your furniture."

She replied, "That isn't mine!" and hung up. I did not hear from her again. Several months later her mother-in-law called and asked if I would rent to her daughter, the daughter's boyfriend and a child. I declined. There is a rather complicated set of laws regarding the keeping of possessions. Study them.

**

When a tenant tells me that they don't have the rent, my favorite line is to tell them, "I am very sorry for your problems, but my banker won't let me pay the mortgage with that story."

I had one tenant tell me that she did not have the money and she had a toothache. I told her that if she did not pay the rent, she would not only be homeless, but she would be homeless with a toothache.

I have had them tell me that their mother was in the hospital. I point out that they still must have a place to live and the fact that their mother is in the hospital has nothing to do with the rent.

One landlord was told, "I had to bury my ex." He told her that her ex had a home, but she would not have one unless she paid the rent.

They will tell you anything to evoke sympathy.

**

THE RENTAL ROLLER COASTER

I rented to a couple who both worked at a large box company. I thought it would be a sure thing if I had to take legal action. Wrong again! I went to court and got a judgment for several thousand in damages. I tried to have them served. The manager said, "Both of them are no longer employed here." You can file to collect on their income tax return, but it is complicated and you have to keep refiling. You don't know how much it rankles. I wish we were allowed to put photographs of the damage along with the driver's license in the newspaper, but alas, we cannot.

***

When you go before the judge, you must remember that he does not know you and everything he hears is for the first time. Rehearse what you are going to say so that you can see where you might need to explain things more deeply. The protocol dictates that you get to speak first. Explain thoroughly, without rambling. Some judges are patient or interested and will listen. Others are impatient and want things briefly stated.

***

I had one professional renter show up in court with a binder full of pictures showing a pristine house that anyone could move into. They did not jibe with the pictures that I presented. When the judge called me to the bench to look at the tenant's pictures, he asked me if this is what the house looked like. I said, "Yes sir, when they moved in it looked like that." They had their kids in court to testify but the judge would not allow it. They also accused me of terrifying the children by driving by the house and yelling at them. I don't yell.

***

Section Eight Housing has told me that I only have two weeks to report any damages for which I have not been paid. If not reported in that period of time, the tenant will be entitled to another house, paid for in part or whole by the government. I have never had a tenant come back and pay me for damages in order to get another HUD house. I have no way of knowing how they got another one: Use another person as the primary tenant, or move to another county?

***

HIPA. That is the Federal law which states that personal information cannot be given out by doctors, postal workers, government workers, utility companies, etc. That is why tenants will cruise the house from which they have just been evicted, get the mail they want and leave the rest. No forwarding address. They will also have the utilities turned on in the name of someone else. Frequently in the name of their children, since all children must now have a Social Security number. The kids end up with bad credit before they even start school, sometimes.

***

Always make sure that the utilities are on. You can do this with a phone call to each utility company.

Here would be a good place to insert the story of Lulu.

Lulu the Laundress

As is my custom, I did a landlord drive-by on one of my rentals. I found what appeared to be a blazing campfire under a tree in the front yard. The lights were off in the house, the front door was open, and a flycatcher was taped to the door frame. Several guests were gathered around the fire. They did not appear to be roasting hot dogs or toasting marshmallows.

This caused me great concern because of the proximity of the fire to the tree, and the proximity of the tree to the house. I called the Fire Department to check on the legality of this activity. I was told that as long as the fire was "not too large" I had no cause for a complaint. Sooooo...

Another drive-by and I noticed that there were several five-gallon buckets sitting around the yard. Not under the tree and not surrounding the fire. Studying the scene more closely, I noticed that the buckets were right-side up. This is not a very comfortable position if the buckets are intended to be used as seating. I called the tenant's brother. I will call him Edwardo. When I asked

Edwardo why there were so many buckets in the front yard, he explained that they were doing their laundry.

I then asked why they did not use their washing machine. He said he did not know and suggested that maybe it was broken. I am a little slow to catch on sometimes, but I finally did. I called the Electric Company and they said that they had shut off the power to the house.

I called the water company and was told that the water had been turned off. I did another drive-by and noticed that a hose was draped over the fence between the neighbor's house and theirs. They apparently were using the neighbor's water (which is illegal). What a sleuth I am! I immediately called Edwardo and set up a meeting with him.

I told him that I would post a Thirty Day Notice instead of a Seven Day Notice if he would promise to have his father and sister removed in that period of time. We shook hands on this agreement. I could have posted a Seven Day Notice but since they were on government assistance and only received one check a month, it would have been useless to try to move them out any sooner. Also, it takes a least 10 days to get on the court docket and the judge will usually give them seven days to move. See how the math works? When you run up against these types of things, always pause to think about the legal ramifications. Sometimes discretion is the wisest action.

Postscript to the story is this: The inspector in charge of fraud for the Power Company called me to investigate "the improper use of the electrical equipment." He informed me that the power had been turned off at the pole.

Apparently, Lulu the Laundress and Luis the Liar (her father) had removed the glass case from the meter and somehow jumped a wire so that the power was on but did not read on the meter. My heart jumped because the law reads that if the power is turned off at the main power pole, which the Power Company had done, I could be required to do a complete upgrade of the electrical system. This could have cost me several thousand dollars.

I explained the situation I had with the tenants and that I had given them a Thirty Day Notice. The investigator expressed appreciation for my cooperation and hung up. I talked to Edwardo. He promised to have them out of the house by the fifth of the following month. We shook hands and I told him that I depended on his word as a gentleman. It turned out that they had used another person's identity to turn on the electrical service. When I got them out and called to have the power company turned back on there was not a problem and no call for an upgrade to the electrical system.

Thank You! Thank You!

Chapter 9

Stoves and Dryers

I had a newly purchased house that was not vented for a dryer and the tenant said that it was not a problem because she did not have a dryer. Since there really was no room for one in the laundry area, I was not concerned. I told the tenant that if she wanted to get a stacking washer and dryer to let me know and I would have it vented. The other option was to put a dryer in the closet in an adjoining bedroom. This is why I did not automatically put in a vent. I was trying to accommodate the tenant.

She soon complained that there was mold in the house, and she was getting sick. I inspected the house and I found mold growing behind the furniture. She had not vented the dryer, which she had installed, and the humidity in the house was so high that everything was slightly damp. This only took about six weeks. I told her that I would have it vented.

Instead of asking me, she had her boyfriend punch a hole in the plaster wall and stick the vent pipe outside. They put a full size dryer in the tiny laundry area and were then unable to open the back door.

These types of tenants are unfriendly and don't want you in their house. I respect that up to a point. I used to assume that they would report any damage that actually affected them. This is not true. When you have as many homes as I do, and work full time, it is difficult to add the additional chore of visually inspecting every nook and cranny of every house on a regular basis.

***

I have one house in which the stove is within about four inches of the wall on one side and the refrigerator on the other. I put up some PVC shower wall to protect the wall and make it easy to clean. In order to fry things, the tenant used such a large pan that it touched the wall. She actually melted the panel. I then replaced it with a cement board. Maybe I should have purchased a smaller frying pan for her. I don't know.

***

For various reasons, some tenants will heat the house with the oven. I believe it is because they do not want to pay the deposit to the Gas Company. The oven is not intended for this purpose, and it will burn out the igniter element or thermostat. This will require an appliance repair person unless you are handier than I. This will not overly worry your tenant because you are required to provide them with a working stove if it is in your contract.

My policy is to fix it once and then tell them if it happens again, I will not fix it and they can either pay to have it fixed or I will evict them.

Always write a letter to them explaining this and keep a copy in your file. You might try appealing to their own sense of self preservation. I tell them that it also releases carbon monoxide into the house and could make them very ill or kill them. This is sometimes enough to prevent problems. Of course, if it is an electric stove, this will not work. I have had several stoves which required replacement after they moved out. I had an electric stove burn up this way.

***

I also had one house where I exchanged an electric stove for one of gas, but not before she had burned up the bake element on the electric stove. She called me to say that the oven did not work. I met the appliance repair man at the house. After a thorough inspection, he gave me his considered opinion in private. I started asking her questions about her use of the oven. It was then that all of this information was revealed.

Here was my analysis. Everything in the house was electric except the heater. The tenant did not want to pay a gas bill year round so she had the gas turned off in the spring. When winter rolled around again, she was heating the house with the electric stove.

When I got the house back, I had the repairman exchange my electric stove for one of gas. Almost all tenants cook so I knew that the next tenant would leave the gas utility turned on. Never sleep! Just keep thinking and thinking. That is the only way you can even hope to keep up with them. You will never get ahead of them. There are more of them than you. They have more experience in these things. I think they have meetings. I don't know where. Stay alert!

***

Speaking of stoves- and I was. When I have cause to move a stove or repair or replace one, I always put in a long flexible gas supply line, so I don't have to contort myself to reach the shut-off at the back of the stove. That way you can pull it out to work on it or clean under it.

All of the houses I have purchased have had short gas lines which means that someone has to lean over the stove to reach the shut-off or move things around. To my way of thinking, it is easier to install a longer line. Don't be afraid that the tenant might crimp the line when they clean behind and under the stove. They won't. The only one who is going to clean under the stove is you or your cleaning people and they won't move it unless you insist.

***

I had another couple move in and use the stove to heat with until they burned up the regulator in the stove. I ended up buying a new stove because my appliance man said that the stove was old and needed a few things which would cost more to fix than a new stove. It worked fine until they started using it as a heater.

***

I had one bizarre incident several years ago. A woman applied to rent one of the houses. She had two teenage children and one child about age 10. When her boyfriend unloaded her things, he unloaded a stove. Since I furnish a stove and refrigerator, she asked if I would store it. I agreed.

The children started school and everything seemed all right. Then she called to tell me that they had no hot water. I went to check on it and found that the TP on the hot water heater was open in overflow mode, running constantly, and had flooded the living room carpet.

Since one of the teens was lying on the floor watching television, I asked why I had not been informed of this before it became such a problem. The child looked up at me and said, "Oh yeah, Mom told me to call you."

I asked where his mother was and was told that she was out of town. The next month I could not get hold of her to collect the rent. After several trips to the house, it became obvious that she was dodging me.

I finally posted a Three Day Notice of Non Payment of Rent Notice. Remember that landlords do not evict. Only the judge can evict! I then got a call from the mother, stating that she was moving and wanted her stove. I told her that as soon as she paid the past due rent and I did an inspection, I would turn the stove over to her.

I next heard from an appliance company in another town. They told me that she had not made payments and they wanted their stove back. I told them the story and told the lady that I could not turn over a tenant's property to anyone but the tenant.

The next phone call was from a television news reporter. She said that she had gotten a phone call about a slumlord situation and that she had gone to investigate. The reporter said that the ceiling was falling down in the bathroom (It turned out that they had hooked the water hose to the evaporative cooler and left the water running), the house was filthy and there appeared to be several teenagers and a disabled ten year old living there without supervision. I said that I would call the police about that.

The reporter, sensing a story about slumlords, asked for an interview for the evening news and threatened to put this mess on the air and make me look bad if I did not comply. I explained the situation to the best of my knowledge. I told the reporter that I would give her the names of my other tenants as character witnesses but that if they or I ended up on the news, I would file a lawsuit.

I explained that I did take very good care of my tenants and the houses. She then volunteered that there appeared to be something wrong with the scene when she went to investigate. Apparently, there were several teenagers living in the house without supervision.

When I finally got them all out and went to clean the house, a neighbor volunteered the rest of the story. Apparently, the mother had a new boyfriend who did not want the children, so she brought them to a town ninety miles from where she lived and rented my house for them.

The postscript to this story is that two weeks later, there was a two part expose about bad tenants and bad landlords. My name was not mentioned.

Chapter 10

The Yards

I don't know what it is about hose washers. If one turns up missing, the tenant will not go to the hardware store and buy another one. They will let the hose, or hose bib, leak and drip until there is corrosion on the metal pipe rising out of the ground and a lake at the foundation of the house.

They will then complain about cockroaches and expect you to take care of them. I am not required by law to do that, and it is in their contracts that they are to manage rodents and insects. If I owned multiple units, it would be my responsibility. I keep washers in my bag.

***

Speaking of bags. One of my children gave me a bag that resembles an old-time doctor's bag. This is one of the best gifts I have ever received.

***

I tell new tenants that I don't care so much what they do in the backyard, but they are to water and care for the front yard because that belongs to the neighborhood. I figure that half is better than nothing, right? I think this is a fair compromise for someone who does not want to take care of my property.

I tell them that nobody wants to look at junk and everyone wants to be proud of where they live. This is not necessarily true but that is what I tell them. This is a constant battle with some tenants, and I deal differently with each tenant, depending on the situation and tenant.

I have had tenants say to me, "It isn't my house, why would I take care of it?" I have been known to mow and sweep the sidewalks of the disabled or elderly. Some in my support group would rather maintain the yards and sidewalks. This was not an option when I was working and now I am disinclined to do other people's lawns.

***

I evicted one family and as I was cleaning, I took a break and sat in a chair by the front window. There were large juniper bushes blocking the view of the street so I could not figure out why there was a large notch in the side of the mini blind. I peered through the hole and found that it showed a direct view of the alley across the street.

This also explained why there was a large gap cut out of the greenery. I don't know if that was a security measure or for watching the path taken by friends or business associates. I later found sixty dollars tucked in those trees. This was the only time I ever found money.

***

One time, during a drive-by, I discovered that same greenery was brown on three sides on the one bush closest to a neighbor. It was still green on the yard side of the bush. The neighbor's side, the front, and as far as someone could reach without coming into the yard, was dead. They had asked me to cut down the tree and I refused. It was totally on my property.

They apparently took things into their own hands and used poison or some such chemical to try to kill the tree. I went to the seed store and asked what their recommendation would be. I was told to water it vigorously for a long time. I did and it finally revived.

***

I purchased a house that had been well cared for by the previous owner. This presupposes that the original owner actually lived in the house, of course. The yards were well manicured, and the shrubbery was shaped and pruned. I decided to pay the water bill for the new tenant in order to encourage her to actually water and care for the yards since there was a large investment in shrubbery, trees, and roses.

It is in all of my contracts that tenants water and care for the yards, although most will not do so unless urged, inspired, or threatened. The tenant who rented the house promised to care for the yards, front and back. There was a sprinkler system in place with a timer that could be set for the optimum time to water the yards. I carefully went over this with her and her teenage sons.

As is my custom, I drove by to check on the house. You can tell a lot about what is going on by checking out the backyard, in particular. I noticed a pool of water on the lawn in the front yard and stopped to investigate. The tenant immediately appeared outside, (hmmmm), talking and gesturing. I asked why there was this standing pool of water. She said that one of the boys had run over the sprinkler head.

She told me that she planned to fix it but had not had the time. I told her to get it fixed immediately and reminded her that the contract stated that no one was to park on the lawn. I pointed out that I was paying the water bill. I also pointed out how easy it is to keep a yard nice when you have a sprinkler system with a timer. I later went by to check on the repair. It had been done.

A few weeks later I again did my drive-by. Yes, landlords do drive-bys, too. I found water running down the street a block away. My fury overcame my normal sense of prudence. I went home and got my reciprocating saw and some plumbing supplies. I then went back to the rental, turned off the water, and using my saw, cut off all of the pipes to the manifold, which went to different sections of the front and side yards. I then capped them.

When the tenant called to complain that the sprinklers did not work, I told her what I had done and told her to water manually and that if she did not, she would be in violation of the contract.

***

Tenants never own a hose. They usually have wide screen televisions and expensive cell phones but no hoses, rakes, shovels or other yard tools. For my own peace of mind, I sometimes provide them.

Fred the Fire Fiend

I get very nervous in the fall when the leaves cover the yards. Most tenants tell me that they rake them when they quit falling. It is hard to make them understand the importance of keeping up with the job. I don't tell them that it creates a fire hazard. No sense in giving them any ideas.

Fred the Fire Fiend began setting fires in the big dumpsters in the alley. Someone was setting them all over town. The Fire Chief told me that he was making arrangements to have cameras mounted on the power poles so they would have proof of who was starting fires.

The trash collector moved the receptacle behind my back fence after the second one had been set on fire and burned up my next-door neighbor's fence and part of mine. Because it was placed next to my gas meter after they came by to empty the dumpster, I used my pickup to push it down the alley to the first chain link fence I could find. This was very unpopular with my neighbors, but it seemed preferable to blowing up the neighborhood.

I called the city department responsible and suggested that they not put the receptacles in front of gas meters. The usual response if you try to talk to the workers is, "That's not my job." Those who don't get paid to think, don't.

A cold front came through and almost all of the leaves fell in one night. The next day I raked up the leaves because the house was empty and there was a storm coming in. I raked up several bags of leaves. During the night the wind blew down more leaves which swirled in the corner of the yard, leaving a small pile against the chain link fence.

The next day when I went to check on the house, that little pile of leaves had been set on fire, along with the trash receptacle in the alley. Had I left those leaves for even one day, Fred the Fire Fiend might have burned down my house.

The Hacker

I purchased one house that had an apple tree and a very large grapevine in the backyard. One summer I gathered nearly one-half of a large yard trash bag full of grapes. I rented to The Hacker. I did not know this at the time. I explained that he needed to water and mow the yards.

Sometime in the fall I inspected the backyard and found that he had cut off one side of the apple tree and had cut the grapevine back, nearly to the ground. I asked the tenant why he had done that. He said that the tree was in the way of his bar-b-que and the kids got scratched with the grape vines.

Explaining that those were mine and that he had no right to damage them fell on deaf ears. I was angry but evicting him would not have brought back my property. Judges will hardly give you damages for houses. I am sure it would be hard to prove damage to greenery. This is why rent houses never look as good as the neighbor's homes.

***

I had one house that I rented to a couple who said that they wanted to buy a house and would have some money for a down payment when they got their income tax check. The house was for sale at the time, so I took down the "for sale" sign and rented it to them with that verbal understanding. I also took my helper to the house, and we trimmed back the large old Chinese Elm in the front yard. I wanted to cut it down, but the prospective new owner said that he wanted to save it for the shade. Since I had cut back the branches and everything looked green and healthy, I left it standing.

After a terrible New Mexico windstorm, I received a call from the tenant, saying that the tree had fallen on their SUV. I immediately went to the house and, sure enough, a long branch had fallen on the back half of the truck. As I stepped out of the pickup a teenage son said, "There's our new pickup." I looked at him and said, "Don't even start that sh..."

The tenant wanted to know if I had homeowners' insurance and I told him that I did, in fact, have homeowner's insurance for my home and I hoped that he had renter's and auto insurance. I reminded him that it is in his Rental Agreement that he should purchase renters' insurance. He had neither. His wife threatened me with legal action and even said that I could expect a call from the car dealership, which held their note. It was one of those "we tote the note" places.

The tenants explained that since the wreck and the DUI, they had not been driving the pickup (not true) and they had canceled the insurance. They then said that the used car dealership was going to sue me. I told the tenant to have the dealership call me. I continued to receive threatening phone calls from the tenant for several weeks, which I ignored. Be tough. Be strong. Never let your guard down.

***

When a tenant is getting ready to leave, they will sometimes seem to withdraw and not be as friendly. You may notice other slight changes like neglect of the property, etc. They may not clean the house or take care of the yard. Don't accept any excuse for non-payment of the rent if this occurs. Otherwise, you may well lose at least a month of rent, along with repairing the neglectfulness.

Chapter 11

Plumbing

Tenants will seldom think to run plenty of hot water down all of the drains. Sometimes they actually pour grease down the kitchen sink. This seems to be a common habit because I have been told by men in charge of cleaning out the main sewer lines in two small towns that sometimes the main sewer lines get stopped up because of this practice.

***

I got a call saying that a pipe had burst in the backyard of one of my houses. I had to be a detective. I had put insulation around the outside pipe, so I knew that it did not burst from the cold. I had used zip ties to hold the insulation. The zip ties were still on the pipe, the pipe was shattered, and the foam insulation was scattered around the yard.It was evident that the dog had torn it up. The tenant swore that she had the dog in the house. I showed her the evidence and told her that if it happened again, she would fix it herself. Stupid is as stupid does.

***

Same house, another time. I was called because the sewer was backed up. I called a plumber and before he even unloaded his equipment, he told me what he would find. The cap had been removed from the clean-out and there was blue water flooding the yard.

Someone used blue mechanic towels for toilet paper. I showed the tenant and told her that if it happened again, it would be her responsibility.

***

Most plumbers will not respond to a tenant's call without contacting you. If one does, you are not liable but if he fixes things with a reasonable amount of competence and for a reasonable amount of money I don't argue. I have had tenants ask the plumber to do things beyond what I have asked to be done. My plumber won't do it without checking with me unless he is reasonably sure that I would want this taken care of in a single trip. I trust him and he trusts me.

***

If I expect really cold weather, I call my tenants and ask them to leave the hot water dripping in the faucet farthest from the water heater. I tell them that if the pipes freeze, they may not have water for several days. This makes it personal with them. The fact that my pipes might burst does not generally concern them. Of course, while it is still warm outside is a good time to winterize.

***

One tenant accused me, in court, of telling her not to use "good toilet paper" and said that I only wanted her to use "the cheap stuff." She proclaimed to the judge that she only used the very best toilet paper. The look on the judge's face was one of astonishment. Apparently, this was one he had not heard of before.

When it was my turn for rebuttal, I explained that most older houses have old cast iron pipes with rust particles in them. Using facial tissue or toilet paper that does not dissolve easily will stop up the drain lines. I can't give you the name of big offenders, but you can do a test with some paper and water and see if it dissolves in the water.

Newer houses have PVC pipes that do not have burrs on the inside. I had named only one brand which several plumbers had also mentioned to me as being troublesome in old cast iron pipes. Tenants can come up with more trouble for you than you can ever imagine. That is why I need my support group. We share the knowledge and the misery.

Chapter 12

Plaster and Sheetrock Walls

I had a house with tall ceilings and picture railings. What is that, you ask? It is a wooden trim that is mounted about one foot from the ceiling. Pictures are hung on wires, ribbons, or straps. This prevents damage to the plaster walls. Plaster is more difficult to repair than sheetrock. I was always very particular about who rented this quaint little house and warned tenants about damaging the walls. I explained how to hang pictures and even offered to hang any pictures for them. If you make a cross of tape and use a small nail, you can usually drive in the nail without causing plaster damage.

An inspection of the house revealed that a large section of the kitchen wall plaster had been peeled off. This was about three feet from the floor. When I asked what had happened, the tenant said that her child had started peeling it and she couldn't get him to stop. I stopped it with an eviction.

Sheetrock

Not much to say here. Either learn to do it or it will be a major expense. Tenants will punch holes in walls. I have noticed that they draw back and tap the wall before striking to be sure that they are not going to hit a stud and hurt their hands. I never saw an indent over a stud.

***

Always put a door stop behind every door. If you don't, you will be patching a lot of holes.

***

In New Mexico, a law was passed a few years ago that a person could not replace more than a two-foot by three-foot piece of sheetrock without a permit. You might want to check the laws in your state. Otherwise, you need an inspector to make sure that there is no lead-based paint.

THE RENTAL ROLLER COASTER

***

You cannot remove asbestos tiles without an inspection and probably a haz/mat team. There are not many of those anymore. They are mostly the nine by nine tiles. The twelve by twelves are vinyl.

Chapter 13

Electric Heaters

Lying Linda said that she only used electric heaters. She said that she did not like to use gas. I explained that electric heaters cost more than gas. This is when I should have called the gas company. She did not have it turned on. The gas company charges a high deposit to turn on that utility if a tenant does not have a good credit rating. Also, this should be noted. The gas company sometimes removes the meter if it has not been used for a while. I have also heard of meters being stolen by tenants to replace their meters which were removed by the Gas Company for nonpayment.

***

I have a very nice two bedroom cottage with a floor heater. Anyone who has ever lived with one will tell you that they work very well but you have to wear something on your feet to keep from being burned. They used to be very popular. They did not have the heater pilot lit. The tenant called to complain that the breaker kept blowing.

I went to inspect before I called an electrician. The first thing I noticed was a large Christmas tree festooned with electric lights. A lighted Nativity scene covered a sofa table and the extension cord trailed from the kitchen into the living room. The television was on as was the DVD player. Surround sound speakers were plugged into the gang plug, to which all the other entertainment items were also connected. The electric stove was warm and no sign of food. In the bedroom was another television, DVD player, a space heater, and more Christmas lights.

I explained that this was an older house and not wired for all that they had plugged in. This is also when I found out that they were heating the house with the oven. They said that they did not know how to light the gas heater. I told them that they would burn down the house if they did not unplug some of their things. It wasn't long before they left. Thankfully!!!

***

I then rented the house to an engineer who worked for the Federal Government. The gas was on when he moved in. He changed the utility to his name and turned off the gas when the temperature rose. The stove was electric. The next winter he wanted me to turn on the heater for him. I told him that it was his responsibility and gave him printed instructions on how to do it and also showed him the small tool that was used to push in the knob. It is lit the same way one lights a water heater. How do you get to be an engineer and not be able to light a heater?

He said that he could not get it to turn on. He soon moved. It cost me four hundred dollars to repair it. I had already settled accounts with him before I found out that he had broken it. I don't know what the solution to that is. They won't pay for a plumber to turn it on, and I am not required to, nor do I want to turn it off and on.

The only solution was for me to hire someone to light the pilot. This frequently amounts to fifteen percent of the monthly rent. I have never had anyone from the gas company who would light it. They are required to light the pilots when a new tenant moves in. Even if the tenant requests that they light the heater they get by without doing this by red tagging it. It does not matter if I have just had it serviced or completely cleaned. This is not honorable, but it is legal.

***

If you allow your tenants to do any repairs, be sure to give them parameters to go by. Some people can barely change a light bulb. Ask for a receipt before you reimburse. I had one tenant give me receipts for some unnecessary things, including a front door. Of course, I did not reimburse him. The old door was still installed. He was always trying to con me. When I went to collect the rent one time, he pulled the cash out of his pocket and handed it to me. When I counted it and told him that he was fifty dollars short, he reached into his pocket, pulled out a fifty and handed it to me without even looking at it.

***

Those tenants who have been with me for a long period of time get a turkey at Thanksgiving. I want them to know that I appreciate them and the fact that they take care of small problems.

**

You can count on this - If a tenant breaks a refrigerator or toilet, and replaces it, they will take it with them when they leave. Yes, they will! Same thing with light bulbs. After all, they bought them. No amount of reasoning will convince them that the toilet is not theirs. They are oblivious to the law that states that if something is affixed to the house, then it must remain with the house, or the house must be restored to its original condition.

**

When someone calls and wants to know if I will accept pets, I tell them that I might if I can see where the pet lives now. No one has ever taken me up on the offer. If you are serious about no dogs, then do what one landlord does.

Drop by the house when you are certain that no one is home and knock on the door. If you hear barking, then you know. The tenant will assure you that they are only taking care of the dog for a friend. This will be a test of how serious you are about your rules. That landlord files for eviction.

**

When you rent a house, always walk through it with the tenant and if he makes any mention of anything, note it on a form you have created for that purpose. If you are smart you will also take pictures and have the tenant sign them. I never did but sometimes wish I had.

**

The best time to find a tenant is August and September. Children are starting school. In January, February, and March, people are getting their income tax refunds and there is usually an increase in the number of people looking for homes. Winter is a slow time because tenants don't like to move when it is cold or during the holidays.

***

The best days to rent are the last few days of the month. People are trying to find a new home before the first of the month when the rent is due. The worst time to rent is the fifth through the twenty-fifth. The applicants tend to be those who have overstayed their welcome and are in danger of or have received a notice of eviction. These are not hard and fast rules, but they tend to follow a trend.

Chapter 14

I Am Not Your Mother And Odd Pieces Of Advice

Some people cannot accept responsibility for their actions. The excuses are endless. Here are a few:

I don't have the rent because I needed shoes, a uniform, and equipment for my job. Translation- Don't you appreciate my industriousness?

I had to bury my ex. A friend responded like this. "Your ex has a home. You won't unless you pay the rent."

I was at a party/had some friends over. My money is missing. -Translation I am a victim of circumstance. Insert grocery store, library, or some other virtuous place to be.

I usually advise them to file a police report. My standard reply is, "I am very sorry to hear that. However, my banker won't let me pay my mortgage with that story so you will have to come up with the money or leave. If you are late there will be a late fee which will create more of a hardship for you."

***

Sometimes the tenants change the locks on the doors and put locks on the gates. It is strictly forbidden by the contract that they signed. This is another reason why I make sure they have read the contract. If I have to call a locksmith or use bolt cutters on locks, they are charged. They will whine and say that all I have to do is ask, but the truth is they sometimes do this, so I do not have access. I never, and I repeat NEVER, enter a house that is rented without notifying the tenant in advance. I have keys that will open all of the houses and if they change the locks, I cannot get in if there is an emergency.

I also ALWAYS go into the house with any service repairman. I don't want them being accused of anything. I am there to help if they need it and spot them on ladders. I also can see that things are done to my satisfaction.

***

If you buy a house with a non-automatic defrosting refrigerator (They are becoming very rare), do not expect the tenant to defrost. If you are fortunate, they will, but when they are planning to leave they frequently will not. I had one couple who left it for so long, knowing that they would be moving, that the freezer door would not close. They apparently slammed the refrigerator door until it broke off the freezer door. Of course, they did not leave a forwarding address.

**

One tenant had three young children and was on HUD and food stamps. I found that she was feeding the kids cold cereal which they spread on the living room carpet. She would then sweep it into a pile behind the front door. I explained how unhealthy that was and suggested that she purchase a vacuum at a yard sale. She said she had no money. I bought her one. In a few weeks, I found out that she had sold it in a garage sale. Not everyone can be helped.

**

On that note, as I said, they sometimes will not leave a forwarding address. What they do is go by and get the mail and then only give forwarding addresses to the contacts they want, such as magazines, utilities and any entity that provides checks, etc. If you want to circumvent this, take the mailbox down. Store it until you have a new tenant. I learned this the hard way.

I evicted one family, and they tied up the dog in the empty lot next door.

They moved out of the house and left a dog, doghouse, food, and water in the lot next door. I put a rubber band on the mailbox to signal the postman that no one lived there. The next day it was removed. I then posted a written notice to the mailman. The next day the note had been ripped off of the post.

I called Animal Control to pick up the abandoned dog. The Animal Control officer came by, but the officer said they could not do anything because there was shelter, water, and food. After a week, I gave the dog to someone, and within a few hours someone from the Police Department called me and asked if I had stolen a dog.

When I explained that the dog had been left tied to a tree in a vacant lot for two weeks, he told me that I had to return it and that the former tenant was going to file charges of theft against me. He laughed and said, "I know those two knuckleheads. There won't be any charges, but you still have to return the dog."

It took me a while to figure out that they left the dog there so that they would have an excuse to get into the mailbox. They only wanted the welfare checks and food stamp authorization, I guess. They left all of the bills and junk mail. Sometimes I am a little slow on the uptake. I subsequently took down the mailbox until I had it rented again. They removed the dog within two days.

***

Another trick that they will use is to leave their things on your property so they can get them at will. Not in the house but in the backyard. I guess they assume that it will take you at least a few days to get around to cleaning up the yard. I remember one family that did this and when I put everything in the trash, which filled up three large alley dumpsters, he came in the night and pulled everything out of the dumpsters and left it strewn up and down the alley. He even threw some of the trash into the backyard. The neighbor across the street saw him do this. I am sure that he was looking for the box of sex toys that I had thrown away. Speaking of which:

***

Whenever I have someone help me clean, I always search the house first, before I have anyone come in to help me. I don't want any surprises. When I finally managed to evict this same family, I went through the house. Upon inspecting the master bedroom, I found several dirty magazines and videotapes. I boxed them up and put the box in my truck then called my helper to dismantle the bed.

He soon came to where I was working, with a very red face, and hesitantly said that I should come to see what he had found. Under the bed was a large box of sex toys. I knew what they were because some of them resembled private body parts. I gathered them and disposed of them in another part of town.

THE RENTAL ROLLER COASTER

***

Check the air vents. I have found some surprising things in them. I like to clean them between tenants anyway, but if there are screws missing, look carefully. I have found marijuana, cigarettes, dirty magazines, food, and other things.

***

If you find red spots on the ceiling, it has probably been caused by people forcing open catsup or red sauce packets.

***

I rented to an unmarried couple who later started to break up. He could not move out without some money for rent and deposit. He wanted the deposit so he could rent another house.

I had a small two bedroom house which was empty at the time. I agreed to let him move into that house, thereby keeping the original tenant and getting a tenant for the empty house. This also solved the immediate problem of who owned the deposit. I later was able to give him a pickup load of furniture.

***

When you have given the tenant a late fee or a fee for damages you have to repair, you can deduct it from the rent that they pay you each month. This will leave a balance owing on the rent. Not paying their rent in full can result in an eviction. This really encourages them to pay their rent on time. Sometimes if you don't charge them for something stupid, they did, they will feel gratitude and may mend the L/T relationship.

One tenant took the lid off of the toilet tank and dropped it in the toilet shattering it. I replaced the toilet without charging her. I could have made note of it and when she moved out taken that off of her deposit, I suppose, although I figure that a tenant who has been with me for several years has earned an occasional pass.

***

At times I have gotten lax about charging late fees and accepting late rent and soon there is an excuse each month. It is difficult to retrain them and it causes hard feelings. You are the adult here so take responsibility for keeping things on track.

***

Make sure that everyone who lives in the house is listed on your lease. If you fail to do this, you may have trouble evicting that person. My contract states that extra people may stay for seven days and then there will be an increase in the rent of one hundred dollars.

***

I make it a habit of driving by the houses at odd times and even driving down the alley. The rental application has a line to list the vehicles that should be there. If I find other vehicles on the property, I take pictures.

I had occasion to do this one time and then I called the tenant and said that I had pictures of an odd car at the house. He said that the person was visiting. I told him there were pictures taken anywhere from five in the morning until after midnight. He knew he was busted, and I got the extra money for one month and then the extra person moved out.

***

One note about posting notices. I use painter's tape and tape all four sides of the notice. I then take a picture of the door. This is legally required of those who serve papers for the court, so I follow their example. I have been able to use this as proof that they were served with notice.

I post in the morning and then drive by in the late afternoon. If the notice is gone, I know they have been served. If they leave it on the door, I wait until I am legally able to post an Abandoned Property Notice. Again, this has come up in court. Cover yourself. Otherwise known as CYA.

***

If there are reasons you need the tenant to vacate, use a Thirty Day Notice. I have been told recently that you are now required to post two notices before you can proceed to court. You do not have to give the tenant a reason although this may anger them. It may also anger the judge. Saying that you are going to sell the house, or your family member is moving in usually works, although I have recently seen on the news (2023) that California may pass a law restricting this as a reason to evict.

Wait until you have gotten the rent, or I can pretty much guarantee that you will not get the last month's rent. They may have enough money to rent another place, but they need to beat you out of your rent to pay another deposit. Here again, if they don't pay the rent on time and you give them a Thirty Day Notice, you will probably lose a month's rent on the back end of this transaction. You are not going to win. Maybe you can keep your head above water. If you paddle like crazy.

***

At the bottom of my checkout list is a notice saying that if they do not comply with the list it may result in garnishment. I usually post this with any notice that I post. For all the good that it does. If the tenant gives me a notice that they are moving, I mail them the checkout notice. Lest you think me unreasonable let me state that they are simple things like taking out the trash, canceling phone service, washing fingerprints off of walls, cleaning bathrooms.

***

One thing that does annoy me is this. I had a rash of rentals where the deadbeats would vacate and abscond with the kitchen drawers. Apparently, they were even too lazy to get their own boxes. I am what I refer to as an extra rough carpenter, not a finish carpenter. I don't like to build drawers.

***

If you have occasion to file for a garnishment of wages, be sure that you know who and where to send the garnishment. I got a court order for garnishment for an employee of a national grocery chain and had it sent to the local store.

I did not know that I had to send it to the head office in Idaho. When I called to check on it, nothing had been done. I was required to file the Writ of Garnishment with the home office.

As I pursued the matter, I found out that the former tenant had two other garnishments ahead of mine. I was later told by the store manager that the former tenant refused to work all the hours that she was offered because that would have meant that the store could take money from her checks for the garnishments.

***

I garnished another former tenant's salary. She apparently did not make enough so the accountant for the company could only take out twenty- five dollars a month. After about three months, she quit, leaving no forwarding address.

***

I garnished yet another tenant's wages. The accountant for that company refused to comply and told the tenant that if he did not pay me, he would lose his job. The tenant came to my place of employment and slammed the cash down on my desk and demanded that I write a receipt immediately. I could have told him to come back but I took the high road, wrote the receipt and he left.

***

When someone moves out, for any reason, remember that you are legally obligated to send a letter of settlement within thirty days. At least this is New Mexico law in 2014. The law may be different in other states. This is difficult if it takes longer than thirty days to repair the damages. If you do not send the letter, you are liable. There are penalties for this. I have heard of landlords being sued and being made to return the full deposit even though there are damages.

If the judge decides that it was willful, he can tack on another $250. The letter is sometimes returned with the address unknown. Save it in the file! If you have a HUD tenant, you only have two weeks, or they will not act on your complaint. I don't know if this is a local procedure or a national policy.

***

An inspection of a house resulted in my finding a drawing of a marijuana leaf taped to the son's bedroom door. I did not think much about it until I evicted them and found that they had turned a storage area into a pot growing room. I then removed the picture from the door and found that it was covering a large hole in the door.

***

There may be other reasons, but I found that these things usually are signs of drug use: multiple bikes and bike parts, with no evidence that they are rebuilding and selling bikes, lots of DVD players and other electronics torn apart, damaged window blinds, usually with a corner cut out at the bottom, braces on the doors, especially back doors and no light bulbs.

I was told that druggies will break the metal end off of a bulb, swish salt or other abrasive around to remove the paint, and then use the globe to cook drugs. Wouldn't want to inhale any paint fumes now, would we?

***

Blood in the refrigerator does not equate with violence. When a tenant vacated a house, I found the bottom of the refrigerator filled with dried blood. Apparently, the meat had been left to drain in the frig. I try to remember that it is a character flaw of the tenant and not a personal insult. I can't help but consider it an insult. This kind of thing will either build a strong character in you or drive you to the edge of sanity.

***

They will take the smoke detectors but leave the bracket that holds them. Have them hard-wired to prevent theft. This costs more money. The funny thing is, they will take the smoke detector and leave the bracket. I guess the former tenant of their next house did the same thing. The round robin of smoke detectors. They are not all the same size.

***

I rented to a couple only to find out later that they scammed a landlord I knew. The first time the tenant called me and told me that she was at the library and her purse was stolen, I had a Three Day Notice Of Failure To Pay Rent posted on her front door before she even got home. She did not bother to call me. Busted! She knew I was on to her. There is an entire story of what it took to get them out. It involved the Sheriff's Department and drawn guns. I told you the story.

The previous landlord had let them get by for several months without paying. When they did finally leave, they took several window air conditioners from some vacant apartments. I feel a certain obligation to stand firm against this kind of people. Failure to do so encourages them to try to cheat other landlords.

***

It just occurred to me that maybe some tenants are like foster children who get moved from one home to another, not knowing the house rules for each house. That does not excuse them from doing the right thing. Just a thought.

***

They will sometimes use the kids and you will look like an ogre putting them out. Remember that they are not yours and the tenant is supposed to take care of them, not you. Once again—-A rental agreement is not an adoption contract.

***

I went to collect the rent at one house and found a very dejected tenant sitting on the front steps. Sad Sack asked me why I was there and I told her that I was there to collect the rent. She said, "You only come around when the rent is due. All you want is money."

"Sad Sack, we are not friends. Our relationship is tenant and landlord. Most people are happy that I don't come around very much."

THE RENTAL ROLLER COASTER

***

One night I was called to one of the houses and found a man in the tool shed. I'll call him Biker. I called the police, but they were too busy to come since it was not a residence, so I accosted the man myself.

He said that he was helping my tenant and that he was living in the tent in her backyard. I called her to verify this. Sometime later she moved, and I told the man that if he wanted to live in one of my empty houses I would furnish the house, utilities, a refrigerator, and microwave for free. I told him I would give him five dollars an hour if he would work two or three mornings a week for me.

He moved in and immediately got sick. Biker was eating food out of the dumpsters. I bought him medicine and brought him food for about seven days before he could work. I helped him get on food stamps. He did not have any ID and since he did not have an address, he could not get the stamps. I got all of that taken care of for him. He would not go to the food pantry or YMCA because he did not want to sit through the 30-minute sermon at either place that provided food. He had a buggy attached to his bicycle.

I gave him the address of one of the houses and told him to paint the cabinets white. I left a gallon of white paint on the counter. When I went by one night to see what he had done, he had painted the cabinets green. In my discussion with him, it became evident that he had picked up the paint in an alley somewhere and thought that if he used it on my cabinets, I would pay him for the paint. I did not. I also did not pay him for his labor.

I also asked to be introduced to the girl who was sitting in the living room, smoking pot. He introduced me. I asked him to meet me at another house in the morning because a sewer was stopped up and I was going to rent a machine and rod it out. He did not show up.

I went to get the rooter and did the cleanout with the help of the tenant. NEVER do this alone. You can lose a finger. One plumber that I knew of was working alone with a rooter and was electrocuted. Never, ever do it alone! It is worth it to call a professional. But I digress.

After we unclogged the line and loaded up the equipment, I headed back to the rental place and who should cross my path but Biker! The girl was sitting cross-legged in the buggy. He waved and continued on his merry way.

It wasn't long before he started hiding from me. I went into a hardware store one day and they asked about him. I said that I couldn't find him. I was told that he had been in there hiding from me the day before. He had told them that I would not pay him to work. They were quite surprised to find out that I was not only paying him, but I was furnishing him a house, utilities, appliances, et cetera, for free.

One time I went to the house to pick him up. I knocked on the front door and called his name. No answer. I went around to the back of the house in time to see his feet disappearing through the bedroom window. When I stuck my head in the window to ask what he was doing, he told me that he was sick.

The next incident occurred soon after this. I went by the house and the front door was open. Inside I could see Biker and another man working on bicycles. The built-in shelves were filled with little trinkets and things that he must have scavenged from dumpsters, such as picture frames, figurines and bottles. The way they were all arranged, it looked like he might have been preparing to open a second-hand store.

I told Biker why I was canceling our agreement. I took their pictures up close and told them to get out of my house. I also told them that if I saw them around my house or if there was any damage, I would call the police. And that was that!

***

If you decide to recover your house for your own benefit, you may be required to give the tenant ninety days' notice. In July of 2023, I heard on the news that California might pass a law making it illegal to evict a tenant for the sole purpose of using the house yourself. I have not followed up on that news.

***

One item in my rental agreement states that the property is not to be used for commercial purposes. That notwithstanding, I have had my houses used for auto detailing, tax preparation, drug sales, and from some of the things I have seen, prostitution. The tax preparer later went to prison for eighty counts of tax fraud.

***

Be wary of the words of a previous landlord. He may tell you that the tenant under discussion is good and that he hates to lose him. He may just be glad to get rid of the tenant. I have had this happen to me. I have even had landlords admit this as though it was a helpful hint. Why do I bother trying to lift up the reputation of this industry?

***

I have become more resigned after all these years, as have some members of my support group. Now we tell each other, "At least nothing is torn up and there are no holes in the wall." Our lives have been reduced to this. They have worn us down.

Chapter 15

Building Trust

I tell people, "I won't lie to you, and I won't lie for you." Sometimes the tenants want you to lie to HUD about things. I have been offered food stamps and have had people offer to buy me groceries with their food stamps in return for their rent. Of course, I refuse. I also will not let someone live in the house if they are not on the lease. Sometimes this is hard to prove.

***

I inspected one house and found a load of men's blue jeans in the washing machine and a pair of men's underwear on the floor of the bathroom. But the tenant swore that he did not live there. I have a problem being a party to tenants deceiving Section Eight Housing by saying that they do not live with someone when they do.

***

In Chaves County, if the owner of a property does not have a Utility Disclaimer on file with the Water Department, he or she is liable for all water bills created by the tenant. I had an occasion where the tenant was evicted, and I later received a letter from the Water Department stating that a lien of two hundred and fifty-six dollars was being filed against one of my properties. I asked the caller why they let the tenant go for three months without a payment. She did not have an answer for that.

I told the caller that I had a disclaimer on file with them. The disclaimer states that I, the owner, will not be responsible for the water bill of the tenant. She said that they did not have it on file. I suggested that they continue looking because I had my copy. The matter was dropped.

***

When you do an inspection, here are some things to look for: Light bulbs missing. Usually the old-fashioned, incandescent kind. The end is broken off and sand or salt is swished around to remove the paint inside. The bulbs are then used to cook dope. When I was being schooled in this side of life by my tenants, I neglected to find out what is cooked in such a fashion. It wouldn't take much to find this out if you are curious. Broken pieces of a car antenna. The pieces are usually about six to eight inches long and are used to snort drugs. Because the parts or so readily available, you will find pieces lying around the house or on the ground outside.

The ground wire from the breaker box to the ground is missing. It is copper and can be sold for scrap. So can bicycles. I have found piles of torn up bikes stashed in odd places. These things I have learned from oh-so-helpful tenants. They seem proud of this knowledge and if you do not act surprised or judgmental, you will be amazed at what they are willing to teach you. Otherwise, it could be years before you acquire so much knowledge. The first things you need to buy are extra lock sets, double-keyed deadbolts, and a bolt cutter. These things will come in handy later on.

***

Clive called to tell me that his house had been broken into. I don't know why he wanted me to drive the twenty-five miles to comfort him in the middle of the night. He was retired from the military and belonged to a church. You would think that he would have better resources than a landlord.

It turns out that he had backed his car up to the house in the middle of the afternoon and loaded his suitcases, thereby announcing that he was going on vacation. Not very clandestine, was he?

When he got back home the front and back door had been kicked in. He seemed shocked that a locked metal chest, about eight inches by fourteen inches had been stolen from the top shelf of his closet. He showed me the master bedroom closet.

His remark when he gestured to the empty space was, "I kept it up here. It was locked. They stole my gun and five thousand in gold certificates." Well! I thought to myself, it was locked after all!

So.... I repaired two exterior doors and fractured door frames and installed wire mesh on the back door window. I told the tenant that he could leave without notice. He elected to stay and install a security system. Someone from his church was supposed to answer the call if it went off. That person never seemed to be available. I was next on the list, so I was called several times to meet the police when the alarm went off. He had usually forgotten to latch a door when he left the house. Sigh!

***

I rented one house to a woman with two children. I knew that she had moved in a boyfriend, but she denied it. She was on HUD. It is difficult to make them follow the rules of my Rental Agreement when they have a government contract. HUD does not seem to enforce the occupants' rule.

The boyfriend, here in after called Gutless Wonder, had his last name tattooed across his back, from shoulder to shoulder in three-inch letters. His real name, not the one I gave him. Why? I don't know. Maybe so that he could be identified if he was found face down or running away.

It wasn't long before I got a call, in the middle of the night. Gutless said that someone had crashed through the wooden fence in the backyard. This is a six-foot, plank wood fence, not a picket fence. I had just finished rebuilding it about two weeks before.

"Was anybody hurt?"

"No, but the car stopped halfway in the backyard."

"Have you called the police?"

"No."

"Why not?"

"Because I called you."

"Why did you call me?"

"Because it's your house."

Realizing the futility of this conversation, I called the police, got dressed, and drove twenty-five miles to the house. By the time I got there, the police officer had made the inspection and talked to the tenant. I spoke to the tenant, examined the damage, and told her when I would have time to repair it.

The officer asked that I step to his car and pretend that we were discussing the report that was attached to his clipboard. He mentioned the man peeking through the blinds and asked what I knew about him. I gave him Gutless Wonder's real name and told him what I knew.

The officer said that he was pretty sure that he had identified Gutless as a drug dealer who was out of jail on parole. The officer said that he thought that Gutless was selling drugs out the back gate in the alley. The officer asked me not to speak about this to anyone. I don't know the end of the story. They moved shortly after that.

***

Same house- different story. I rented to Rock Man. He had buckets of rocks and stacked them by the wooden fence in the backyard. He also had lots of electrical tools in a makeshift shop in the den. I believe that most of them were for polishing and cutting rocks.

One fine day when he was away, someone broke into his house. Rock Man's dog chased him off. Rock Man called me. I went to inspect. Following the footprints and other traces, I figured out what had happened. The thief had pulled forward into the driveway. The entire front of the property was enclosed in chain link fencing. He had then re-positioned his car at an angle that would be the most advantageous orientation to hide his dastardly deeds.

He hopped over the locked, backyard gate. Because of the metal screen I had installed on the back door after the former last tenant's break-in, he was unable to break the glass and reach in and open the door. He therefore kicked it in. Meeting him there in the kitchen was the tenant's dog.

Fearless Fido chased the would-be thief. Rather than take the time to scale the gate, he stepped on buckets of rocks, turning them over and leaving footprints in the dirt. He then grabbed the gate post and swung over the fence, tearing one of the top fence boards loose and detaching the post from the fence.

I don't know if the dog followed him. I did not see any more of Fearless Fido's tracks. The thief then jumped in his car and pulled forward to align his car with the open gate in the driveway. In doing this, he hung a bumper on the chain link fence surrounding the front yard. I am sure that by now his heart was racing as he backed up, pulling my chain link fence with him.

Soooo... I now had to repair the back door and frame, replace the gate post, repair the top of the wooden fence and replace about thirty feet of chain link fence.

Postscript to this story- You can only appreciate this if you have ever had to replace a chain link fence. It is not too difficult, normally. You attach one end of the chain link fencing to the post, unroll the fencing, and place two boards (two by fours, at least five feet long) on each side of the fencing and bolt them together. Then you tie the cable of a come-a-long around the two-by-fours and attach the other cable of the come-a-long to your trailer hitch. Start cranking and soon the fence lifts up, and you tie the fence to steel posts which you replaced the day before by setting them in concrete.

The reason it is the day before is because you have let the cement set up so the posts will stand upright. So far, so good. The reason this was problematic was because I had to park in the street, on a busy corner, in order to get the angle right for pulling the fencing tight. If I could have found the little pinhead, I might have beaten him with one of the mangled posts.

The tenant had to pick up his rocks.

***

The next tale of woe is another fence story. Maybe I should have put in a chapter about fences. I bought a house and inherited a tenant. She was fragile mentally, financially, and in other ways. She was on HUD, which explained why she did not work. She had two children. Her father lived with her. The cinder block fence and chain link gate had been damaged, so I worked on it several weekends (remember that I had a job)and finally got it repaired.

***

Over the next several months, as I did drive-bys, I noticed that the fence and gate were being damaged. I talked to the tenant about this, and she said that the neighbor kids would damage it as they walked by. Of course, no one tried to stop them or make a police report.

After she moved out, I found out that I now owned a drug house. I also found out that the dad was selling drugs out of the back yard. Funny that the neighbors never tell you anything until after you have gotten rid of the problem. I had no idea there was so much activity in the alleys!

***

That reminds me of another incident at this house, with a different tenant. I had a mother and three teenage boys in the residence. The neighbor across the street showed up at my place of employment and complained that there was the sound of a slamming door at about two o'clock every morning and it woke his wife, who "snored so loud that she never woke up."

I called on the tenant and found out that she was slamming the door trying to get it to latch. Upon examining the door, I found that it had been kicked in. When I asked her why, she said that one of the boys had been locked out, so he kicked it in.

Postscript- After they moved out, another neighbor told me that the kids climbed in and out of the windows breaking the aluminum frames on five of them. Since there were eleven windows and I could not find any to match, I had to purchase and replace all of them.

***

Speaking of those windows. They were Vinyl-clad, double pane, low E, white. Very nice. I had a helper and we had to cut the windows out of the stucco walls, install new windows, re-stucco, and paint the exterior to match the rest of the house. Then we removed the trim on the inside, insulated, replaced the trim, and painted.

The front window was tricky because it was three windows combined. Beautiful.

I describe all of this so that you might feel the pride and satisfaction I felt in the looks and workmanship.

Sooooo- I rented to another woman with two grandchildren that she was raising because the father, her son, could not provide and the mother was in prison. Son lived with his mother. Son had a girlfriend. Son made Girlfriend mad, so Girlfriend picked up a brick from the walkway and heaved it through the front window.

Refer to the end of this book. I have enclosed a Landlord's Prayer. I told the tenant that she would have to pay for the custom-fit window. She did. I then got to replace the brand new window, again.

***

Same house, different tenant. I got a call from a woman with two teenage boys. She wanted to rent the house. I told her that I was taking applications, but it would not be ready to rent until I finished tiling the bathroom and doing some plumbing in the kitchen. She assured me that she did not care about that but that she needed to get her furniture moved out of her previous apartment.

That throws up red flags. I checked her credentials, the best I could. She worked for her father, at his business. I let them move in with the understanding that my cleaning lady and I would be coming in and out.

As I came into the house in the late morning, I was surprised to find four bodies wrapped in blankets. The discarded shoes and tousled hair protruding from the cocoons indicated that they were probably teenage boys.

No amount of noise disturbed their slumber. For a few days, they arose around noon. One thing that puzzled me was the large red Coke machine and two large coolers placed in front of the house. A pool table was in the den. I noticed several footprints on my newly painted wall. Apparently, the little hoodlums stood around the pool table with their feet propped on the wall. So cool.

I went one morning to tile around the tub with twelve inch by twelve inch sheets of mosaic tile. Someone had used sheetrock compound to attach the tiles in a haphazard manner to the wall. Fortunately, the compound was still somewhat wet, so I was able the scrape the tile off of the wall.

I then spent the morning soaking them in buckets of water, trying to get them clean. When I rehung them with mortar it was like trying to paper the wall with worn out dish rags. No one knew who could have committed such an ignorant act.

My cleaning lady could speak Spanish and repeated some things she overheard, which gave me cause for concern. After a short period of time, she was able to tell me that they were selling drugs out of the Coke machine and coolers. I don't know if they were selling anything that had to be refrigerated. Do any illegal drugs have to be refrigerated?

I found that they had turned on the gas at the meter, without having ordered the service. Of course, they had free water because I was still working in the house. The only utility the mother had turned on was the electricity. I called the Gas Company and reported it. They locked the meter. That and the fact she did not pay the rent, as agreed, gave me enough reason to evict her.

Postscript to this story- I knew that there were people going to the house looking for drugs because the neighbors told me, after the fact. What did I do? I put up a sign that said the teenage boy, Salesman, (who was supposed to live there) had moved. His new phone number was XXX-XXXX. I listed the number of the police station. The next day I found that someone had come by in the night and scratched out the number with an ink pen. Sometimes I do have a little fun with them. :)

Chapter 17

And So You Did What?

This may be my favorite chapter. I have stood in front of tenants, dumbfounded and in absolute disbelief at some of the things that they have done. I try to keep a calm demeanor and maintain a neutral look on my face so they will tell me the truth. That is, after all, the only way I can find out what really happened so that I can go about mitigating or repairing the damage and maybe prevent it from happening again.

***

Sometimes my heart pounds at how close they have come to losing their lives, and even blowing up my houses. The following is a prime example. This incident cost me several thousand dollars. Let's call him Bonehead.

Bonehead did not pay the gas bill, so the Gas Company turned off the service to the house. Bonehead then turned it back on. The Gas Company locked the meter. Bonehead cut the lock. The Gas Company then removed the meter.

Bonehead then did the most frightening thing you can imagine. He took the cap off the main gas line and installed a piece of pipe to bypass the meter, which puts Natural Gas directly from the main line into the line leading to the house. The gas line, which runs down the alleyway, is under several pounds of pressure. The system is designed with a regulator at each meter which then siphons around eight to eleven ounces of pressure to each domicile. The tenant therefore put the pressure of the entire gas line into the line going to the house. My heart still pounds at the thought of what could have happened!

I did not find out about this until I evicted them. I noticed that there was smoke damage on the ceiling and walls of the kitchen. I also like to test the utilities, to make sure the tenant has not done any damage. When I called for a reconnect of service, the serviceman for the Gas Company was unable to light two of the three wall heaters in the house.

When I called for service, the serviceman related to me all the activity which had taken place at this address. He told me what they had done, explaining the pressure that had been exerted on the lines. This also blew out the regulators in two of the three heaters. It cost me several hundred dollars to replace those. He left the gas turned off because of leaks in the line.

Then the plumber did a test on the lines, as required by law under these conditions. It is a two thousand square foot house which started life as two separate houses. They were connected by a twenty-foot hallway, with bedrooms along the way. The house stretches from the street on one side, nearly to the alley on the other.

After finding and repairing several leaks, joint by joint, the plumber said that it would be more economical to bypass all of the old lines and replace the entire gas line. It ended up costing me a couple of thousand dollars. By the way, it also costs to have the line tested, which the Gas Company requires before they will provide service to a home. The thumping you hear is my heart. It still pounds when I think of it.

***

I recall one family that I inherited when I bought a house. They afforded me no end of amusement and fear because of the things they would do. Let's call them Wannabe Gangsta' and Missing Marbles.

Marbles complained about some things in the house, so I went to investigate. The easiest to fix were the "rust spots" in the bathroom. After I examined the ceiling, I determined that they were not rust spots but stains from the cigarette smoke which combined with the moisture from the shower to make spots on the ceiling. I told them that if they opened the window when they showered, they would not have this problem. I also suggested that they clean the ceiling and do their smoking outside.

***

The next complaint was that the bathroom door was falling apart. After studying it, I determined that they hung wet towels over the door. The moisture from the towels in the humid environment of the bathroom caused the glue holding the laminated door together to separate. I showed them that wet towels had caused the white stains on the door. It also caused the door to delaminate. Why they did not use the towel bar is still an unanswered question.

***

The next complaint was that Marbles, and the kids were sick all of the time and she had headaches. I brought a carbon monoxide monitor to the house. The reading was well within the safety parameters. I mentioned the fact that Wannabe was sitting there with perspiration running down his back. It was so stifling in the house that I could hardly breathe.

I left and bought a thermometer and placed it in the dining room. I told her that I thought the headaches were a result of the house being so hot. She denied this. It was winter, but winters are normally mild in New Mexico.

I went back the next evening to check the gauge. When I asked Marbles where it was, she pulled it from behind a decorative plate which was in a glass enclosed, built in, China cupboard. It registered eighty-five degrees. She did not believe me when I told her that I thought that the heat and lack of fresh air circulation was making them sick.

I then showed her the carbon monoxide monitor as proof that she was not being poisoned. I told her that the next time she took the children to the doctor, she should tell him that she kept the house at eighty-five degrees. Our tax dollars at work.

***

The next incident started when Wannabe called to tell me that his feet hurt from trying to dig up the front yard, so he could plant grass. I told him that I would buy the seed and rent a rototiller to turn the ground. We settled on the following Saturday for this to happen.

On Saturday I thought it would be a good idea to check on Wannabe before I rented the rototiller. I knocked on the front door and heard a weak, "Who is it?" I announced myself and was invited in. Wannabe was wrapped in a blanket, lying on the sofa. He was pasty colored and bleary-eyed. It was obvious that he was very hung over.

"You poisoned yourself last night, didn't you?"

"Yeah." he moaned.

"Well, shall we try for next Saturday?"

"Yeah."

***

The next time Wannabe called; he said that the smoke alarm kept going off. I went to the house and tested the alarm. It appeared to be in working order.

"When does the alarm go off?"

"When Marbles cooks."

"What does she cook?"

He pondered this question for a while before he answered.

"Grilled cheese sandwiches."

I moved the device from the kitchen to the hall, a distance of about five feet in that tiny house.

Again, the phone call.

"The smoke alarm keeps going off."

What was Marbles cooking?"

"Spaghetti."

"OK. I'm going to call an electrician and be at your house tomorrow."

I told the electrician that I wanted a ventilation fan installed directly over the stove and while he was at it, I wanted one installed in the bathroom. Older houses like this one had windows in the bath and kitchen, designed to be opened for ventilation. Obviously, this was not done.

The electrician said that he was going to connect the fan to the overhead light. He then asked me to flip the switch so it would not have power to it while he wired the fan into it. I flipped the switch, and nothing happened.

Wannabe said, "Oh, you have to wiggle the switch to get it to turn off and on."

"Why didn't you tell me about this, Wannabe?"

"Well, it's no big deal. We just wiggle it until it turns on or off."

I shut off the power at the main breaker.

115

When the light fixture was pulled down so that he had room to connect the new wires, we saw that the wires were frayed and burnt several inches from the connection. I pointed this out to Wannabe and Marbles.

Marbles then said, "You know, the light bulbs never last very long in that light. Sometimes we see pretty blue balls rolling around in the glass."

There was total silence as the electrician, and I looked at each other. I don't know about him, but my heart nearly fell out of my chest.

***

The next time I went to collect rent from Wannabe I found the outside light fixture hanging by the wires. I knocked on the door and Wannabe answered. I gestured to the porch light.

"What happened here?"

"I was going to put a dimmer on the fan light in the living room."

"So, why did you disconnect the porch light."

"Because all the wires are connected right here."

He gestured to the gang box beside the living room door. I tried to explain the nature of the connections but was met with a blank stare.

"I will tell you again, Wannabe, Do Not work on my house. If there is a problem, let me know, but Do Not work on my house, OK?"

A slow nod, which I knew did not mean yes, followed.

***

The next incident was more hair-raising than any that went before. I was at work and received a phone call from Marbles. She was very excited and said there was a fire in the house. I asked her where and she said that it was "coming from the pipe by the heater." I told her to get everyone out of the house and I would have someone up there immediately.

I called the plumber. He dropped everything and went to the house. From there he called me and said that there was an eighteen-inch flame emitting from the supply line which was no longer attached to the free-standing heater in the living room. He said that he turned off the gas and was going to go get the parts to fix the damaged copper supply line.

I then called Marbles and asked her what happened. She said, "Wannabe thought he smelled gas, so he told me to go borrow a pair of pliers from my mother. Then he took the pipe loose from the heater, but he still smelled gas, so he took the pliers and bent the pipe." What she meant was that he crimped the supply line, the same way that you crimp a hose to stop the flow of water.

"He said that he still smelled gas, so he took his lighter and when he lit it, it went Whoosh!"

I told her to stay out of the house until it was fixed. I next received a phone call from the plumber. He said that while he was gone to get some copper tubing, Wannabe had removed the heater and it was standing on the front porch, along with all of the ductwork that had been pulled from the ceiling. The plumber then said that because of this he would have to re-build everything to bring it up to code. It is an old house.

I called Marbles back and told her what was being done. When I was presented with the bill, I called Marbles and scolded her for what they had done and told her, once again, not to work on my house.

The next day she called me back and said that she and Wannabe had gone to the hardware store and priced the piece of pipe that he had broken.

"That guy cheated you. That pipe only cost eight dollars. If he charged you two hundred, you shouldn't pay it." (2007.)

"Marbles, do know what it means to "grandfather in?"

"No."

"It means that when that heater was put in, it was legal. The plumbing code allowed the heater to be installed the way it was. When Wannabe took out the ductwork and removed the heater, the plumber had to go by the new laws. That is why it cost me so much. Do Not work on my house!"

***

I got back at Wannabe one time. After we put in the new grass, he wanted something to put around the yard to keep people from walking on it. I installed pieces of rebar and some yellow caution tape. From a distance, it looks like the tape that police use to mark a crime scene.

It wasn't long until I got a call from Wannabe.

"I took down the yellow tape. My friends gave me a hard time about it. It looked like the cops were here."

I knew they would. That's why I did it. :))

Why did I let them keep living in my house? I liked the little dumbasses, and I was concerned about what might happen to them. They stayed in my house, on HUD, for a couple of years and then bought a house. I saw them last year and they are doing fine.

***

Always take plenty of pictures before you begin to clean and repair. Witnesses are a good thing to have. This is where your support group comes in.

***

If you buy a house that turns out to have a bad reputation or if a tenant turns out to be a bad tenant, especially a criminal or drug dealer, it will be necessary to select as the next tenant one who knows the score about these things and knows how to handle it. Let him know ahead of time what the situation is and let him know that he has your support. I usually reduce the rent a little. It makes us a team.

***

I recall one such tenant. He was nearly as wide as he was tall. I will call him Turbo. I am sure that he could bench-press a refrigerator. He had multiple tattoos and face piercings. In spite of his appearance, we struck up a friendly relationship. He did not mind the reputation of the house and was able to run off the people who came around looking for a former tenant.

He told me one time that if I needed help, to call him. He offered to collect the rents if I was having trouble. He told me that now I had "people." Sometimes it is good to have people.

***

One man asked to rent one of my houses. I gave him an application and told him that I was only taking applications at this time. He had notches in his eyebrows, tattoos and refused to make eye contact with me. Go with your gut in these situations. My dog even growled at him. She was a good judge of character. The thing that bothered me was the fact that he did not make eye contact.

I did not feel free to discuss the scary clown with feathers and jagged knives tattooed across his chest. That is not to say that you should not rent to people like this. I still smile when I think of Turbo. When you are alone in the world it is nice to know that you have "people."

Chapter 18

Helping Tenants

When I was looking through my old files to find items for this book, I found some things that I had forgotten. Looking back, I can't believe that I was so naive and went so far above and beyond what I probably should have done. I know that part of it was because I had it within my power to make a difference in the lives of those less fortunate. Sometimes it is hard for me to find the balance between charity and enabling.

***

Normally I don't like to start a sentence with the pronoun "I." This next part is just to let you know that I am not a heartless monster, regardless of what you might have heard ;).

In the course of my land-lording career, I have:

1. Purchased a cheap car for a tenant. The tenant worked it off.

2. Allowed a woman to move into a house who had just gotten out of jail for embezzlement. She could not get her children back unless she had a house. I am a soft touch for children and old people. After an interview, I told her that I would rent the house to her. In her excitement and appreciation, she hugged me, ran outside, jumped in her car, and promptly backed into my pickup.

3. Composed and paid for the printing of business cards so a tenant could advertise her business of yard and house cleaning.

4. Composed and printed the resume for a tenant who was looking for a job.

5. Bought a set of tires for a man who worked for me. His were bald. He worked off the debt.

6. Purchased a used laptop for a tenant so her daughter could spend more time at home instead of at the library, doing her homework.

7. Supplied a house and utilities for a homeless man and then fed and nursed him back to health after he ate food out of a dumpster.

8. Paid my mechanic to look at a tenant's car and found out that it would cost more than the car was worth.

9. I don't remember why I have a letter from that mechanic to Magistrate Court stating that he was not able to fix the car economically and I had offered to pay

for another car for the tenant, if he could find one for a certain amount of money.

10. Paid for a battery for a tenant who struggled to pay her rent each month. When she said that she did not know when she could pay me back, I told her to pay it forward.

11. Took a tenant's son to Walmart and bought all of his school supplies.

12. Showed up in court as a character witness for a tenant so she could be released after a psychiatric evaluation. Her lawyer pled with the judge to release her. The judge said no. Then her lawyer told the judge that I had agreed to be responsible for her. She was released.

13. Loaned several tenants money. They usually paid me back.

14. Forgave some rent when a long-term tenant lost his job.

15. Acquired a complete houseful of items, from forks to furniture, for a family living in a van at the park. I then installed them in one of my houses and gave him a job helping me remodel. And the list goes on.

Nearly every one of these kindnesses came back to bite me. I did these things to remind myself of my humanity in this insane world. It brings to mind a line from the Garth Brooks song The Change. "What I do is so, this world will know that it will not change me."

Chapter 19

Please Lord I Need Your Help

Looking back after twenty years in the business, I can honestly say that the vision does not match the reality. If you have any idea that you are an honest, upstanding citizen with a kind heart who is more than willing to help someone, spend a day in Magistrate Court on the days that the landlords come in.

I know that they all felt or feel the same way that you will; that you are an honest, upstanding citizen with a kind heart who is more than willing to help someone. Spend a day in Magistrate court on the days when the landlords come in.

I can guarantee that when you leave the courtroom you will be convinced that they are all liars, cheaters, drunks, and just plain mean. Of course, you will doubt yourself too.

When someone asks me if they should get into the rental business, the image that comes to mind is the movie in which Jack Nicholson screams out, "You can't handle the truth!" If you get into the business, you will have to be smarter and tougher than you are now. Those who don't make it through this boot camp will probably have rentals for sale, cheap. Look for these people. I found several houses this way.

One word of counsel that you should keep close at hand is this. Worry is a circle of inefficient thoughts, whirling about a point of fear. Get a handle on exactly what is upsetting you. Your support group can be a big help with this.

It is said that God looks after fools and children. I think he sometimes looks after landlords too. If you still think that being a Landlord is something you want to try, I am happy for you. The world needs landlords. They are a special breed. Best wishes to you. If you need a model prayer, I offer this:

Landlord's Prayer

Father, grant me patience. Quickly, please. I am very angry, and I seek your peace and wisdom. Please keep one Hand on my shoulder and the Other over my mouth. Most of what I want to say will not help the situation. Let me always be mindful that I will have to explain my actions to a judge and to You.

Please give me strength and endurance. I need both. Help me to remember why I chose this profession. Bring to mind my good intentions. Help me, please, Father, because you know that I don't want to end up in prison over this. Amen

My Final Tenant

One tenant lived in one of my houses during the rental moratorium. He lived there without paying rent for five months while I was out of state in a rehabilitation facility after fighting for my life due to a massive infection.

The tenant went through my packed and stored belongings. He stole over ten thousand dollars' worth of tools, clothing, jewelry, feed tubs, and livestock watering tanks. He was seen going through my things and burning what he did not want.

He stole antique light fixtures, a door, and a fan out of the house. Those were the things that I remember.

I talked with my attorney, and he offered two directions that I might take to eject the tenant. He said that he did not have much confidence that either would work. He also said that he would require a five thousand dollar deposit to begin proceedings.

The way that I was able to remove the deadbeat and his family was to send him a demand letter stating that I would file for garnishment of his wages if he did not pay me and vacate. I don't know if that would have worked during the moratorium, but he moved.

The Federal moratorium was lifted in August 2021. New Mexico did not lift the moratorium until February of 2022 at which time they moved to an Eviction Diversion Program which effectively put evictions on hold while more legal wrangling took place. Many landlords had mortgages on their properties. Some of them were hurt beyond recovery.

I was able to save my leg and my life by getting the care I needed out of state. By considering the theft of my belongings and lost rent as a cost of getting well, I am able to regard those fifteen thousand dollars as a medical cost. It saves my peace of mind. I am grateful for my life and the doctors and family members who cared for me during that trying time.

I have published a book of fiction, The Other Side Of The River: a story of love, war, cattle and cowboys. I am immensely proud of it. I have also published the book that you are now reading, The Rental Roller Coaster.

I have other books that I am working on. I also write short articles on Medium and Substack. The covers of both books and my website were designed by Poindexter Designs.

My website is sandraallensworth.com/. I hope to see you there.

About the Author

Sandra spent 58 years in South Eastern New Mexico before retiring to Middle Tennessee.

She spent her working years in the field of interior design, ultimately purchasing seventeen houses in a little over six years. She was able to remodel, repair, and refurbish these abused and neglected homes, turning them into rentals. These homes were ultimately sold on Real Estate Contracts, resulting in the successful retirement that she enjoys today. It took time, a credit card and various skills to accomplish this. She has now collected some of her experiences and solutions into this book.

Read more at https://sandraallensworth.com/.